RIPPLES

of

HOPE

Thoughts on Raising
Children to be Hopeful in
Our Changing World, and
Questions to Ask Ourselves

KATHRYN PEPPER

ISBN 978-1-09833-560-1

PREFACE

As a teacher who has taught for thirty-six years, I have been blessed with many opportunities to teach children fundamental values within an integrated curriculum; that includes the study of different countries and cultures and our own history as a Nation. Our curriculum is broad and comprehensive and teaches children to: think for themselves, learn to make decisions about what they believe, and to think about how their actions and choices determine who they are and who they will become.

My original intent in writing was to provide a guide for parents to help them with home learning. As the events happening in our country evolved, my purpose for writing began to change and became a stream of consciousness with an urgency to connect how the continued history of oppression and social injustice in our country, magnified by the effects of Covid-19, created a precipice for change and positive action. It has created an opportunity to not only investigate and embrace our own biases and our role in racism, but to use what we learn to help raise our children to be hopeful.

When raising our girls, my husband, George and I knew it was vital that we help them be compassionate, optimistic, resilient, determined, hard working, and independent thinkers. Most importantly we taught them to be kind and treat others with respect and thoughtfulness. It was also important that we taught our girls to look beyond themselves and not only to have empathy for others, but also to take action to help others and to stand up for what is right, both for themselves and for others.

Now, they work diligently to make a difference as they teach, create and coach. They make us extremely proud as they positively impact and guide the lives of those they mentor with integrity, resolve, high expectations and kindness.

Our family believes Confucius' words, "If you think in terms of a year, plant a seed; if in terms of 10 years plant a tree; if in terms of 100 years, teach people." (1) We believe in the potential of all people!

INTRODUCTION

"Never argue with stupid people, they will drag you down to their
level and then beat you with experience." (2) Mark Twain

S tupid is not a very nice word, though it is concise. Throughout my life, I
have tried to learn from both my positive experiences, and my mistakes
as a person, a mother and a teacher and not repeat things that turned out
to be stupid.

Currently, we are experiencing the biggest change of our lifetimes—
we are trying to make smart choices to protect our families, others, and
ourselves. We are trying to adjust to the new information and expectations
and just trying to adjust to a new way of life.

While safely sheltering at home with my family during the quaran-
tine implemented to help slow the spread of the Covid-19, I am using the
extra time I have to write. When not preparing Seesaw lessons, Zooming
with my students, or updating the parents from our small school with
informative (and hopefully inspiring) messages to help them cope with the
current situation and uncertain future we all face; I am working hard to
create a balanced life. A life that includes an appropriate dose of science

and facts from the news to help comprehend and digest the immense tragedy this virus has caused our families, our nation, and our world, without feeling completely hopeless and terrified; and a life that includes an appropriate amount of normal activities. I am also trying to mitigate the guilty feelings I feel in my "normal" time, as I work in the garden, or ride my bike with my family and somehow feel unaffected by what is happening. I marvel at the fact that my plants are thriving, my flowers are blooming, as heartbreaking events continue just outside our fence. Each night, I feel the need to know the number of souls that have passed that day and pray for their families. I pray for all those who are facing this head-on everyday: for our doctors and nurses in hospitals who care for the sick, for our E.M.T.s who care for those on the way to the hospital, for our leaders, for our scientists working on a vaccine, for our inventors for creating ventilators with new materials, our armed forces for building hospitals, for those in the grocery stores stocking the shelves each day, for those in post offices delivering our packages and letters, for those delivering our groceries, for our trash collectors keeping our areas clean, for our truck drivers who deliver goods for our everyday life, for our teachers working to teach children remotely, and for all the others I have overlooked.

Common vocabulary helps everyone understand concepts. *Flatten the curve* in the past might have meant daily sit ups or a strict weight loss diet, now it means physical distancing, washing your hands, staying home when you are sick, wearing a face mask, giving your packages and groceries a bath, and vigilantly disinfecting surfaces.

The use of the words *vulnerable populations*, though not new, hit home quickly with me, since my husband, George, raises his hand three times during, the television commercial about those more vulnerable to Covid-19, (age, cardio history and cancer survivor) and how to ensure their safety.

Vulnerable populations typically include the economically disadvantaged, racial and ethnic minorities, the uninsured, low-income children, the elderly, the homeless, those with cancer, HIV or compromised immune systems, and those with other chronic health conditions, including severe mental illness, as well as, rural residents who have difficulty accessing health care services, due to education, income or lack of insurance coverage. (3)

This pandemic has unearthed our failure to protect the vulnerable populations. Many of us have a choice to stay home and safely shelter in place in our homes, with electronics, healthy food, books, games and activities that make this time feel like an extended (albeit isolated and slightly terrifying) vacation. Currently, there is an insightful commercial on television by Kia Motors *Accelerate the Good Program*, about how the homeless face this pandemic, with these powerful words,

"How can you shelter in place when you live on the sidewalk? How can you wash your hands for 20 seconds, when you don't have soap and running water? Right now it makes it tougher for America's homeless youth…so to combat this, Kia is giving another million dollars to help the homeless youth." (4)

If this doesn't make us reevaluate our current circumstance and our ability to continue to shelter safely in place for as long as necessary, I am not sure what will.

It is clear that America's vulnerable populations need our help and maybe this help and additional support begins in schools.

Throughout the years, schoolteachers, nurses, administrators, and social workers have taken on more responsibility in raising the children of their community. Schools have taken the role of feeding children, counseling them, supporting them with after-school programs to help them with homework and enriching their lives with activities, games, and discussions.

The children who seem to be having the most difficulty with remote learning, are often already behind academically. Maybe if we can support their parents, their parents can learn to support them more effectively. This process may begin by helping parents close the academic gaps they may have themselves, providing resources and internet connections and then by helping them to obtain and receive adequate medical insurance, and eventually helping them find employment that mirrors school hours and maybe a job within the school system with a component that includes a learning opportunity.

This time that we spend apart from each other, flattening the curve allows us time to examine our values and ask ourselves, "What responsibility do we have to help and protect our vulnerable populations?"

While in the midst of a global and novel pandemic outbreak, our country faced another horrific death at the hands of police while people watched helplessly, unable to elicit change with their shouts. I pray for the families of all citizens who were murdered due to the color of their skin. I pray for their friends, for our country, and for all who march peacefully to protest these deaths in the midst of a pandemic that is disproportionately killing people of color. I pray for the safety of people during these protests as senseless violence explodes around them. I pray for God to guide families through the everyday challenges of determining what is next as they help their children feel normal and safe as they begin to navigate a path and purpose through this "new normal" we are facing.

As I lie awake for long periods of time at night and my body tries to get a good night's sleep, my mind tries to solve the problems of the world; while also trying to determine how education will look in the future for the children who attend our small school.

The balance we seek is delicate and unique to each one of us. Writing has helped me to process and make some sense of the impact of this virus, and the impact of racial injustice and hate on daily life. It has prompted me to think about how we can learn from history, and use our experiences to teach and raise children with strong values who are hopeful in a changing world.

As you help the next generation understand the current injustices and continual racism that are so prevalent throughout our country, I hope that you will also teach them to remain optimistic and resilient. I hope these stories and thoughts about the collision of Covid-19 and racial injustices (Part 1: Change), ideas about teaching your children values through children's literature (Part 2:Values), thoughts for teaching your child at home (Part 3:Thoughts on teaching) and ways we can generate change (Part 4: Pause and Resolve) will be helpful. As you digest and better understand the historical and current events of our country, it may help to remind you that education is broader than classroom walls. Education is life as it happens and we are all learning together. We all need to do our part to create a better, safer world for the future. We need to dig deep and examine our character and our actions to determine how we can be an inspiring example of hope and change for our children.

PART ONE:

CHANGE

How will we fight for the kind of world we want for our
children and what will that world look like?

PERCEPTION

When we look at a situation, our response, feelings and actions to the situation come from our perceptions. Our perceptions come from our experiences, our upbringing, our education, our beliefs, our values, our culture, our race and our community.

Seven Blind Mice by Ed Young (5) is a children's book about seven blind mice that encounter a strange "Something" near the pond. As each mouse visits and investigates the "Something", they determine it is a 'fan', a "pillar", a "spear", a "cliff", a" snake" or a "rope". Until finally, the last mouse runs along the "Something" from the front and back, from tip to tail and all around and realizes it is an elephant. Like the mice, our perception is distorted when we see only part and not the whole, but when we see things from all sides, our perception may be clearer.

Our perception of Covid-19 changes how we look at this deadly virus. Those who view this disease as a disease that only kills the elderly, or those with underlying conditions or the poor and if they don't fall into those categories; may feel unaffected by this disease and continue normal life, without a mask, and without physically distancing from others. Just as those who feel unaffected by racism and injustice may not think racism presents a problem for them and unfortunately are not willing to work towards or recognize the need for reflection and change.

When we think about our perception of prejudice, discrimination and racism we need to remember that these acts and feelings are hard for us to accept and understand from our limited view. These perceptions are also based on our experiences, our upbringing, our education, our beliefs, our values, our culture, our race and our community. Prejudice is bigger than us, but part of us and woven into the fabric of who we are. When we have prejudice, we prejudge someone with an often unfair and unfavorable opinion. Many times this judgment comes without any knowledge or information about them or can be based on stereotypes, misinformation or fear. This prejudice can define who we are, but **thankfully it does not always define those who we are prejudiced against, though as they internalize this prejudice, it may cause them to feel inferior.**

Discrimination: by definition is when we act on our prejudice. When we treat people differently based on their race, religion or their affiliated group we are discriminating against them. This discrimination may result in people being mistreated, bullied, belittled, oppressed or ignored. When discrimination is based on the color of a person's skin and supported by people in authority, or people who hold the power in our society, and these prejudices permeate our laws, our government, our educational systems and how we police our communities. Then the discrimination becomes racism, and is supported by the invisible structure of oppression. Racism is embedded in our culture.

As we respond and react to the most recent deaths at the hands of police officers that have pledged to serve and protect us, the protests, the violence and the urgency for change; we have to remember that our experiences and our perception of the circumstances are different for different people. People are protesting for many reasons. They are protesting for systemic change, for equal treatment, and for accountability for people's actions. They are protesting for equality for all people and for changes in how police officers react and interact with people of color and the force they use. When facing police in full riot gear rather than police who are present to protect the protestors, another layer of emotion and fear is added and the perception is changed. With changed perception, we have a change in our reaction to events as they unfold. Do we feel threatened or do we feel protected?

I listened to a police veteran of ten years explain his fears of dying on the job and leaving his family without a father. His worry for his children's safety and the impact of the horrors he has seen has made him decide to leave the police force. As I listened to his story, I was struck how his fears are parallel to the fears of men and women of color, whose worry is about dying due to the color of their skin. How they worry about their children's safety and how the impact of the horrors they have seen determine their perception of the world. These stories are intrinsically linked together. The solution to these problems is also linked together. It's real conversations where communication can happen.

We all need to look at our perception of how we view the current and past events of our country. We need to ask ourselves are our perceptions clouded by animosity, anger, jealousy, fear or racism? Can we learn about and understand the feelings and the plight of others? Can we understand how the depth of racism affects the lives of others, without feeling the effects of racism ourselves? Can we reflect on our actions and actively work to understand, identify and lessen racism in ourselves? Can we become anti-racist and work against racism? Communication may lead to understanding. Understanding may lead to change.

Books about Acceptance and Perception for children:
Friends by Helme Heine

I'm Not Just a Scribble by Diane Alber

The Big Umbrella by Amy June Bates

Strictly No Elephants by Lisa Mantchev

The Perfectly Perfect Wish by Lisa Mantchev

HOPE AND ACTION

"Actions express priorities" Mahatma Gandhi (6)

Our Kindergarten curriculum covers many topics that have a common thread of hope and action. We study different cultures and countries not only to learn about the history of our world and our country, but also to understand the situation a person or people were in that caused or elicited an action. We study customs, religions and traditions to make connections between history and current events. We learn how the choices and actions we take can change or have the potential to change the outcome of an event. We learn how actions can protect a community or group of people, and how hope can change the path or how actions can sometimes cause upheaval and chaos. We study history, because we should and because we learn through history.

We also know that history usually repeats. If we are aware of the events that positively or negatively altered events in the past, we can take action to avoid the path that leads to repeating negative events.

Albert Einstein's quote echoes this thought, "We cannot solve our problems with the same thinking we used to create them". (7)

Eleanor Roosevelt's soup kitchens during the Great Depression, was an action that gave hope to the hungry.

Women marching for the right to vote or the right to be heard are actions founded in hope for a positive change.

American, British and Canadian soldiers storming the beach of Normandy, France to liberate Western Europeans from Nazi control during World War II, provided hope that allies working together can protect humanity and make a positive change.

Martin Luther King Jr's peaceful marches, speeches and protests were actions to expose the inequality and unfair treatment of people of color with the hope that these marches would make a positive change.

We need to have hope, but we need to take action that will change our path. I believe that any positive action that you take can make an impact. You can take actions to be a healthier person or a person with more patience as a parent or home educator. You take action to be a kinder friend or a more thoughtful neighbor. You may also choose to take action to become a more accepting citizen, a person who can stand with another in protest even if you haven't felt what they feel. I think these types of positive actions will give you hope.

Books about Hope for children:
Tikvah Means Hope by Patricia Polacco

I Can Hear the Sun by Patricia Polacco

The Last Dragon by Susan Miho Nunes

A Chair for My Mother by Vera B. Williams

Owl Moon by Jane Yolen

The Purple Coat by Amy Hest

Miss Rumphius by Barbara Cooney,

The Raft by Jim LaMarche and

Sylvester and the Magic Pebble by William Steig

FINDING YOUR VOICE

"Darkness cannot drive out darkness: only light can do that. Hate cannot drive out hate: only love can do that." Martin Luther King, Jr. (8)

Currently, in the midst of this global pandemic, we are facing another horrifying example of the problems our country and world face; with the disgraceful treatment of others due to race, religion or beliefs. Our country is ravaged with the same scenario that has played out over the past 401 years. The catalysts that drive these evil events are similar, though the names and geography have changed. This catalyst is hate, deep-rooted hate, passed down from generation to generation, and fostered by words, actions and tweets. This hate festers and spreads like an unseen disease. We are all shackled with the responsibility to resolve and repair the history of hate.

In the words of Fredrick Douglass, "No man can put a chain about the ankle of his fellow man without at last, finding the other end fastened around his neck." (9)

The first African slaves were brought to our country in 1619 when the ship The White Lion, brought 20 slaves, to the British colony of Jamestown Virginia. (10) Those 20 slaves had been stolen from the Portuguese slave ship, San Juan Bautisa that was headed to Mexico. The collective "we" in American today were not slaves or slave traders. We do however; have the responsibility be part of the solution to the problems and injustices and continued ramifications, biases and actions slavery still causes today both socially and economically. We have to understand our biases and our role in the system of oppression in order to change. We have to find and lift our voice to object to injustices and then really listen to those who face those injustices. We have to listen and learn.

I have experienced bias, but I have never experienced racial discrimination. I have never had someone cross the street to avoid walking by me. I haven't been stopped by police and worried for my safety. I have never been called a racial slur. I have never had to worry about the safety of my children because of the color of their skin.

Current senseless black murders spurred by hate and injustice, bring a cross section of American protesters out to march peacefully in a pandemic; many without face masks, and many endangering their lives to use the power of their voice to call for change.

As buildings and businesses are destroyed and ignited, violence clouds the clarity of the peaceful fight for justice.

Finding and using your voice should never endanger your life. We have the right to be heard, the right to have an opinion and the right to protest peacefully. I am not sure how the right to voice your thoughts, opinions, frustration and anger; turns into an opportunity for another group guised as protestors to torch and burn businesses and incite more violence.

Our voices should not be for hate, but to be heard as we fight for anti racism and equality, as we fight for justice for those without a voice or a voice we have ignored for so long.

John Lewis, long time Civil Rights Activist and Congressman, raised his voice as he addressed the people of Atlanta, Georgia when he said, "We must continue to teach the way of peace, the way of love, the philosophy and the discipline of non-violence," "And never, ever give up on any of our brothers and sisters. We're one people; we're one family. "

Lewis also said, "To the rioters here in Atlanta and across the country: I see you, and I hear you," "I know your pain, your rage, your sense of despair and hopelessness. Justice has, indeed, been denied for far too long. Rioting, looting, and burning is not the way. Organize. Demonstrate. Sit-in. Stand-up. Vote. Be constructive, not destructive. History has proven time and again that non-violent, peaceful protest is the way to achieve the justice and equality that we all deserve." (11)

Babies are not born with hate in their hearts. They learn hate, from being exposed to hate, from witnessing hate, from hearing hateful words. Hate in our country has been both open and cloaked, exposed and suppressed, encouraged and admonished. Hate is raw, senseless and pure evil. I know a person whose behavior and words can be abrasive and hurtful, but they can also be very kind and loving. I am not sure that their anger, spitefulness and rudeness is based and rooted in hate, but maybe it is based in unhappiness or exposure to hate growing up. Through the years some of the abrasiveness has been rubbed off and smoothed away and replaced with a more balanced, more thoughtful attitude; but that hate and admonishment can appear quickly and easily. There is still more work ahead and I use my voice and actions to help promote kindness and help smooth those rough edges, but I usually stand dumbfounded with my mouth open as a response to the hateful words. I need to be brave enough to continue to find my voice.

When I was little, we had a Rock Tumbler. You could find an ugly rock and put it in the container with an abrasive substance that I don't recall what it was and then put the thick rubber bands around the container to keep it closed tightly. Next, you put the container on the machine and it would turn endlessly for maybe a month. As it turned it made a great grinding noise that was so loud it was always moved into the garage. As it tumbled noisily in the garage we would check on it and cross off the days until we could open it. When the magical day finally arrived, we would all excitedly await the results. As we took out the rocks, they were covered with a gray, gritty substance and as you wiped them off you exposed an exquisite, and extraordinary rock. The rocks were so beautiful we used them to make rings, necklaces and bracelets and proudly wore them.

Our hate is like that ugly rock that needs an aggressive approach to wear away the darkness. We need uncomfortable conservations. We need open discussions that expose our feelings, our anger, our heartbreak, and our pain, to find our hope. We need to shed light on and talk about history with children in schools and at home, we need accurate accounts of our painful history in order to teach our children to push out hate and replace it with acceptance, empathy, understanding and love. We need to be the example of love that our children need.

We may find a cure for this virus, but will we find a cure for hate? We need a concerted effort of working together.

Books for Finding Your Voice for children:
Sit in: How Four Friends Stood Up by Sitting Down By Andrea Davis Pinkney

Bully by Patricia Polacco

Nelson Mandela by Kadir Nelson

Our Future: How Kids Are Taking Action by Janet Wilson

This is How We Do It by Matt Lamothe

HIDDEN FROM VIEW

George Floyd's death became the catalyst for action and change, not just in Minneapolis, but also around the world. His death was the tip of the iceberg. The rest of the iceberg lies below the surface, hidden from view and includes other injustices and mistreatments that have occurred since our country's beginnings: to Native Americans, to Asian Americans, to Jews, to people who suffer from mental health issues, to people whose opinions are different, to the under educated, to the poor, to the neglected, the abused, and the silenced. People are raising their voices for change, and they are raising their voices to be heard. Many people are questioning George Floyd as the face of this movement with prior arrests, but this was the critical moment for change. His life mattered.

Claudette Colvin, at the age of 15 refused to give up her seat, on a Montgomery, Alabama bus, nine months before Rosa Parks, but leaders thought a woman would be a more relatable representative for the civil rights movement than a teenager. So Rosa Parks became one of the faces of racial injustice in Montgomery, Alabama in 1955.

If you keep watching the protests, you see people coming together more peacefully and coming together to sing inspiring hymns and songs like, We Shall Overcome. (12) A song about overcoming segregation and injustices by walking hand in hand, by not being afraid and still having hope that we can live together in peace. This song was inspired by Charles

Albert Tindley's 1901 version I'll Overcome Someday, (13) and transformed during different times in history to better fit the current event. The Bill Withers' song Lean on Me (14) also has an inspiring and hopeful message of unity can also be heard. Singing together does not signal the end of the protests for change. It signals the unifying ability of people from different backgrounds and experiences to come together and overcome injustice while leaning on each other for strength and support.

I think what we can all learn from these peaceful protests is that we are facing an amazing opportunity for a new beginning, one where we can overcome injustices and inequalities by reflecting and exploring racial realities and challenging racism. Whether or not you agree or disagree with this movement towards change, or our path to change, change is necessary. I agree and support the right to protest and support these peaceful protests. We need to have our voices heard, and I pray we can move forward peacefully and productively and lean on each other and learn from the experiences and perspectives of others. Swallow our pride and call on each other, the lyrics from the song, Lean On Me by Bill Withers make this clear.

> *Sometimes in our lives we all have pain*
> *We all have sorrow*
> *But if we are wise*
> *We know that there's always tomorrow*
> *Lean on me, when you're not strong*
> *And I'll be your friend*
> *I'll help you carry on*
> *For it won't be long*
> *'Til I'm gonna need*
> *Somebody to lean on*
> *Please swallow your pride*

If I have things you need to borrow

For no one can fill those of your needs

That you won't let show

You just call on me brother, when you need a hand

We all need somebody to lean on

I just might have a problem that you'll understand

We all need somebody to lean on

Lean on me, when you're not strong

And I'll be your friend

I'll help you carry on

For it won't be long

'Til I'm gonna need

Somebody to lean on…

PROACTIVE STRATEGIES FOR UNCOMFORTABLE CONVERSATIONS

Today, we have the choice to have uncomfortable conversations with our children and as a community about both the historical and current injustices that we face as a nation and a country towards people of color. We need to talk and educate ourselves about the past, our mistakes, the tragedies of slavery, the Civil War, the Civil Rights Movement and the senseless killings that become normalized. We need to talk about the mistreatment and murder of Native Americans, and how Asian Americans were interned in camps after the attack on Pearl Harbor, just because of their ancestry.

We need to recognize how dominant cultures hold power and how this culture, or how white people have historically tried to assimilate other cultures to reflect this dominance and belief. Our dominant culture forced Native American children to attend our schools, to speak English and "assimilate" them into our culture, with haircuts, clothing, education, and also required them to celebrate our traditions, while abandoning theirs. With the decision of Brown versus The Board of Education, (15) we assimilated children of color into white schools, leaving black schools boarded up and black teachers jobless. We separate our communities in cities by buildings and bridges to segregate populations. We continue our dominance of culture in classrooms with curriculum that reflects a white version of

17

history, in theaters with movies that reflect white perspectives and with news that reflects white opinions. We have to make the choice to continue to open up the wounds, and to face the ugliness of actions we have taken as a collective and individual people. We need to begin to understand the role dominant culture has on our society and how it's continual perpetuation by people of privilege benefit from this culture through laws and policies. We need to fight for the kind of world we want for our children. We need uncomfortable conversations to help us begin to understand one another.

Maya Angelo said, "Do the best you can until you know better. Then when you know better, do better." We do know better, let's do better. (16)

On my desk is a paper titled The Ultimate List: Strategies For Oppositional Kids and Young AdultsbyThePathway2success.com. (17)

As I look at it, it struck me that these strategies are extremely useful and concise. These outlined strategies are vital as we begin the uncomfortable conversations and actions necessary to unravel and deal with each strand of hate we have in our country.

It begins with Proactive Strategies:

Build a relationship,

Start fresh each day,

Explicitly discuss expectations,

Develop routines,

Teach social skills,

Teach coping skills,

Identify triggers,

Be consistent, and be aware of your emotions and actions.

In the moment Strategies:

Stay calm,

Use de-escalation strategies to reduce tensions,

Get help to regulate emotions, and Give space and be clear and concise with expectations.

Post Problem Strategies:

Stay calm; reflect on the problem you are solving,

Make a plan together,

Give strategies time to work, and

Forgive and don't give up!

These simple strategies are applicable to solving many of our problems we currently face and if they are successful with children and teens, just think how effective they would be with adults who are ready for change.

Children's books to make a proactive change:

Enemy Pie by Derek Munson

Sticks and Stones by Patricia Polacco

CHOICE FOR CHANGE

We have the choice to be part of the changes we need and help our children live in a world where all people are safe and treated equally. We have the choice to teach our children accurate history at home and demand that it is taught in schools. When looking at the signs the protesters carry, I want more information and more experiences of injustice from the history of our country to be represented and understood. I want them to add Crispus Attucks' name, a former slave who was one of the first to die by the British in the Boston Massacre. People need to know that there were more than 5,000 black soldiers that fought for America during the Revolutionary War. (18) They need to acknowledge the slave uprisings of Nat Turner and Denmark Vesey.

I want them to know about Emmet Till, who was beaten, shot and thrown into the Tallahatchie River with barbed wire and a 75 pound metal fan around his neck for nothing more than talking directly to a white cashier in a grocery store, and to recognize how his mother stood by his open casket to show the world the evil of racism; and help bring attention to the thousands of lynchings that had been happening and ignored for over a century in the south.

I want them to understand how Harriet Beecher Stowe's book, Uncle Tom's Cabin, (19) exposed the unspeakable evils of slavery to the north and was in part a catalyst to the abolitionist movement. I want them to know that the abolitionist movement opened the door for women suffragists to gain the right to vote in 1920, but it took another 45 years with the passage of the Voting Rights Act for people of color to gain the right to vote.

I want them to know that by the end of the Civil War 186,000 black soldiers had fought with the Union forces and 38,000 lost their lives. I want them to know that the Emancipation Proclamation proclaimed that slaves within any state or designated part of a state…. in rebellion… shall be then, thenceforward and forever free, (20) but it took the passage of the 13th Amendment to officially end slavery. I want them to demand and protest until the words of our Declaration of Independence come to fruition: that every person in this U.S has the right to life, liberty, and the pursuit of happiness, and that the government has to listen to its own people. (21)

I want them to know that there is a National Museum for Peace and Justice in Montgomery, Alabama that is a memorial to the victims of 4,400 lynching in the south. (22) I want them to know about Vagrancy Laws, The Southern Manifesto (23) and the effect of Brown vs. The Board of Education, that all these actions and laws renamed and reinforced oppression and racism. I want them to know words from the speeches of Martin Luther King, Jr. and the words of Desmond Tutu.

I want them to know accurate history, so they know the impact their words and protest will have on our future. I want them to know about and honor those who worked and died for change, to provide them the opportunities they have, though flawed. I want them to know they can overcome the darkness of injustice in humanity with their voices.

I know too much information on a sign would cause a conflicting message, so the perfect message is: *Black Lives Matter.* (24)

Bob Marley said, "When darkness surrounds you, you might be tempted to look for a switch or hope that a light comes on to get rid of it all. But you have to remember that you are the light, and you have the power to overcome the darkness that exists in this world. LIGHT UP THE DARKNESS."(25) – I want them to know that they are the light.

Some great books about equality, accomplishment and Civil Rights that we read in school as we study US history are:

Separate is Never Equal by Duncan Tonatiuh,

A First Look at The Skin I'm In by Pat Thomas,

Martin's Big Words by Doreen Collier,

Rosa by Nikki Giovanni,

The Story of Ruby Bridges by Robert Coles,

Jesse Owens, Fastest Man Alive by Carole Boston Weatherford,

Wilma Unlimited by Kathleen Krull,

Pink and Say by Patricia Polacco,

Let the Children March by Monica Clark-Robinson,

Kids Discover: Civil Rights, Civil War, and Abraham Lincoln,

African American Inventors by Otha Richard Sullivan,

Black Pioneers in Science and Invention by Louis Haber,

Art From Her Heart: Folk Artist Clementine Hunter by Catherine Whitehead and Shane Evans,

Young Gifted and Black: Met 52 Black Heroes from Past and Present by Jamia Wilson,

George Washington Carver: The Peanut Wizard by Laura Driscoll and Jill Weber, and The Other Side by Jacqueline Lewis

Questions to ask your child as you read these books: Why is this topic important? How did the book make you feel? What is the author's message? Where do these events go on our chronological history timeline of United States History?

PERSISTENT WOMEN FOR CHANGE

"The Measure of Intelligence is the ability to change." -Albert Einstein (26)

W e are at a turning point in history where we are poised for change. Historically, women's accomplishments, struggles and words are sometimes muted or overshadowed by the voices of others. On the news, someone talked about the number of women yelling to protest the killing of black men, more loudly than black men are yelling.

In countries where women are leaders, their country had fewer cases of Covid-19; due to the sensible action, treatment and tracing protocol that they initiated quickly with solid science based information.

In schools, at times, girls tend to be quieter and well behaved. We need to teach girls the importance of using their voice, to stand up for change and to demand that they be heard. We need to share the achievements of the amazing women who have shaped our history by their contributions.

"Unbought and Unbossed", was Congresswoman Shirley Chisholm's campaign slogan, as she became the first black person to seek the Democratic presidential nomination in 1972. (27) Chisholm knew her chances of winning weren't favorable, but wanted to create a coalition of supporters and influence the winning candidate to focus on rights for women, black Americans and Native people. Running against George Wallace and openly racist from Alabama who called for, "Segregation now, segregation tomorrow and segregation forever."(28), made her campaign more poignant. When Wallace was shot five times, Chisholm realized the danger she faced, but continued on, determined to show the American people what could be accomplished. Her courage and hard work helped pave the way for our country to elect Barack Obama, as the first black American President of the United States in 2008 and Hillary Clinton as the first woman as the Democratic party's nominee for President of the United States in 2016. Unbought and Unbossed!

An inspiring book <u>The Power of Her Pen: The Story of Groundbreaking Journalist Ethel L. Payne</u> by Lesa Cline Ransome, (29) tells about Ethel's persistence and determination to reach her dreams of becoming a writer and journalist. She walked miles to attend a school with white children, amid yells and rock throwing by those who protested her presence. She worked hard and took every opportunity she could to write and expose the ignored stories of the Civil Rights Movement. Eventually, in 1954 she became one of the first African American White House press correspondents. Her questions were direct and focused on desegregation, immigration and anti-discrimination legislation. Her stories on exposing racial discrimination were so impactful, upon her retirement from the press corp.; President Lyndon B. Johnson gave her the pens he used to sign the Civil and Voting Rights Act.

Recently, Congresswoman Alexandria Ocasio-Cortez, was treated disgracefully and called an unconscionable name by a fellow Congressman. His apology was hollow and incomplete. Her response was one that makes parents proud. She emphasized the importance of equality for all people as she said, "Treating people with dignity and respect, that is what makes a decent man. And when a decent man makes a mistake, he tries his best and apologizes, not to save face, not to win a vote. He apologizes generally to repair and acknowledge the harm he has done so that we can all move on."(30) Her statements powerfully resonate the importance of being accountable for our actions and words and that not only a sincere apology for disgraceful actions against all women is necessary, but a change in actions that reflect respect is vital.

August 12, 2020 is a historic day for all women. Kamala Harris, a woman of color, is making her first public appearance as the Vice Presidential nominee for the Democratic Party. (31) Her ancestry is diverse. Her mother is from India and her father is from Jamaica. Her parents met in the sixties during the Civil Rights Movement and marches. Her parents' passion for social justice spurred her passion and as a young girl she dedicated her life to truth and justice. Growing up, her mother told Kamala and her sister that it was up to them to keep on marching for change. With the courage of Shirley Chisholm, and all the heroic women of history, Kamala honorably (though not officially until August 19th) accepted the candidacy for Vice President. In this role she will work to "build a country that lives up to our values of truth, equality and justice"

Throughout Kamala's life, her mother told her don't let anyone tell you who you are, you tell them who you are. She does, she is Kamala Harris- a woman For the People.

Greta Thunberg, an environmental activist, who at 17 years of age is valiant in her efforts to alert us to the dangerous effects on our Earth and our future if we neglect to address and mitigate our impact on climate change. She initiated the Fridays for Future movement, which encourages students to skip school every Friday and "sit in" to demand action on climate change. Last September 4 million people from 161 countries joined her march and used their voices to demand positive action against climate change. She has spoken before the United Nations, US Congress and the

UK Parliament. In 2019, she was Time magazine's Person of the Year! On her 72nd Friday of sitting outside Parliament, she is the epitome of persistence and a testament to the power of a determined, selfless youth fighting for positive change. (32)

We need to teach our children about women in history who persisted and continue to persist for change or those who positively influenced history like: Wilma Rudolph, Henrietta Lacks, Harriet Tubman, Jane Goodall, Eleanor Roosevelt, Rosa Parks, Ruth Bader Ginsburg, Dr. Elizabeth Blackwell, Mother Teresa, Anne Frank, Barbara Walters, Louisa May Alcott, Ruby Bridges, Opal Tometi, Constance Baker Motley, Amelia Earhart, Nancy Pelosi, Hillary Clinton, Elizabeth Warren, Jeannette Rankin, Carol Moseley Braun, Helen Keller, Mala Yousafzai, Kamala Harris, Greta Thunberg, Laura Ingalls Wilder, Clara Barton, Marie Curie, Indira Gandhi, Sacagawea, Molly Pitcher, Michelle Obama, Phillis Wheatley, Ella Fitzgerald, Ida B. Wells, Zora Neale Hurston, Dr. Sally Ride, Margaret Thatcher, Anna Julia Cooper, Billie Holiday, Oprah Winfrey, Patsy Takemoto Mink, Victoria Woodhull, Mae Jemison and Susan B. Anthony and so many, many, more.

We study many of these women in school with the hope to inspire girls to know that historically, women have had the power and continue to have the power to promote positive change. We need to encourage girls to be a persistent voice in their schools and community.

Here are some wonderful books that highlight the struggles, accomplishment and inventions of women and how they have fought for change. It is ironic, however, that women who are changing history are called rebels, bad or daring, but these great books can empower girls and impress boys.

Herstory: 50 Women and Girls, Who Shook Up the World by Katherine Halligan and Sara Walsh,

Fly High! The Story of Bessie Coleman by Louise Border and Kay Kroeger

She Persisted by Chelsea Clinton

100 Women Who Made History: Remarkable Women Who Shaped Our World by DK

Women Who Dared: 52 Stories of Fearless Daredevils, Adventures and Rebels by Linda Skeers,

Bad Girls Throughout History: 100 Remarkable Women; Who Changed the World by Ann Shen,

Anthology of Amazing Women Who Dared to be Different by Sandra Lawrence and Nathan Collins,

Girls Who Rocked the World: Heroines From Joan of Arc to Mother Teresa by Michelle Rochan McCann,

Girls Think of Everything: Stories of Ingenious Inventions by Women by Catherine Thimmesh and

Hidden Figures, The Story of Four Black Women and the Space Race by Margot Lee Shetterly

SMALL DOSES

During this tumultuous time, we can also expose our children to small, controlled doses of information and images surrounding the hateful crimes that are occurring. This is the perfect time to discuss or study the history of similar crimes in our country from the buying and selling of slaves, the Civil War, Jim Crow laws, Redlining and its effects, The East St. Louis Massacre, the bombing of "Black Wall Street", the Civil Rights movement, and centuries of racial injustices. (33)

There are some great books that deal with oppression, injustices and paths to equality. A very well written series on American History by Joy Hakim, a winner of the James Michener Prize in Writing, is A History of US. (34) These books are written for about middle school age, but are great as a read-aloud for younger children or for parents to brush up on their knowledge of United States history and summarize the information for children.

Some great books about our Constitution and The Bill of Rights for upper elementary school children are:

Shh! We're Writing the Constitution by Jean Fritz,

A More Perfect Union, The Story of Our Constitution by Betsy and Guilio Maestro and A Kid's Guide to American's Bill of Rights by Kathleen Krull. Understanding the Declaration of Independence by Sally Senzell Isaacs is a clear, informative book for kids. An amazing book for elementary school aged children is <u>A Child's Introduction To African American History, The Experiences, People and Events That Shaped Our Country</u> by Jabari Asim.

One of my favorite books to read to my Kindergarten class to make slavery current is <u>Freedom over me Eleven slaves, their lives and dreams brought to life</u> by Ashley Bryan. (35) This book is impactful because it provides the perspective of Mrs. Fairchild, the plantation owner, after her husband has passed away and shares her need to sell her estate (which includes the eleven slaves) and the unique perspective of the slaves. Each slave describes their abilities, training and a monetary worth that is assigned to them based on their skills. The amazing part of the book is each slave's narrative that explains their dreams, their quest for knowledge, their hopes and how they long for a proper marriage, freedom and a better life where they live without fear. This beautiful book shows how education and the attainment of skills builds hope for a better life and how love; dreams and hope can never be chained.

Fill your home library with books about diversity like the following and keep adding more books that celebrate both struggles and success of people and how their hard work, discipline and self reliance became an effective way for them change their fate, help themselves and to help others:

<u>Let it Shine: Stories About Women Freedom Fighters</u> by Andrea Davis Pinkney,

<u>Women Voice of Freedom: Fannie Lou Hamer- Spirit of Civil Rights Movement</u> by Carole Boston Weatherford,

<u>Schomburg:The Man Who Built A Library</u> by Carole Boston Weatherford,

<u>Something Happened in Our Town</u> by Marianne Celane, Marietta Collins and Ann Hazzard,

<u>Heart and Soul: The Story of America and African Americans</u> by Kadir Nelson,

Sweet Clara and the Freedom Quilt by Deborah Hopkins,

This Book is Anti-Racist: 20 Lessons on How to Wake Up, Take Action and Do the Work by Tiffany Jewell,

Not My Idea: A Book about Whiteness by Anastasia Higginbotham,

A is for Activist by Innosanto Nagara,

Amelia's Road by Linda Jacobs Altman,

The Legend of the Indian Paintbrush and The Legend of the Bluebonnet by Tomie DePaola,

Crow Boy by Taro Yashima,

Angel Child, Dragon Child by Michele Maria Surat and

Children Just Like Me: A Collection of Children Around the World by Discovery Kids.

Jakes Makes a World: Jacob Lawrence A Young Artist in Harlem by Sharifa Rhodan-Pitts

Ruth and the Green Book by Calvin Alexander Ramsey and Gwen Strauss

Follow the Drinking Gourd by Janette Winter

All Different Now: Juneteenth, The First Day of Freedom by Angela Johnson

The Civil War for Kids: A History with 21 Activities by Janis Herbert

Richard Wright and the Library Card by William Miller and

As Fast As Words Could Fly by Pamela M. Tuck

Henry's Freedom Box by Elen Levine

The Butterfly by Patricia Polacco

January's Sparrow by Patricia Polacco

Make a timeline and record all historical events of our country to provide a chronological frame of reference for your child. Spend time talking about the events of each day, reflect on them, look back to history and see how these events are different or similar to what is happening now and ask what do you think of all this? How does this make you feel? What could we do to change these events? Children always have great solutions and insightful ways to make a change or to make a difference in our world. Children are wise and the answers for our future depend on their understanding of not just the past, but what is important.

STRENGTH

"Strength shows not only in the ability to persist,
but to start over." F. Scott Fitzgerald (36)

We are at a pivotal point in history where we need the strength and the courage to start some things over. The positive result of these tragic events and continuous injustices against people of color in collision with an invisible, deadly, airborne disease has provided an amazing opportunity to help us find our strength and our courage. As a country, we need to dig in with determination to work together to root out, identify and name our many biases, injustices, and prejudices and begin to make amends, to ask for forgiveness, to forgive and to begin to heal the century old wounds peacefully.

President Carter and his wife Rosalynn issued statements about the protests in response to George Floyd's death.

"People of power, privilege, and moral conscience must stand up and say 'no more' to a racially discriminatory police and justice system, immoral economic disparities between whites and blacks, and government actions that undermine our unified democracy. We are responsible for creating a world of peace and equality for ourselves and future generations," he said.

"We need a government as good as its people, and we are better than this."

"Our hearts are with the victims' families and all who feel hopeless in the face of pervasive racial discrimination and outright cruelty. We all must shine a spotlight on the immorality of racial discrimination," "But violence, whether spontaneous or consciously incited, is not a solution." (37)

Our solution is in courage and the strength to start over together. Just imagine if all people; including those with power, privilege and moral conscience worked together to solve the problems of our society? That is strength and power!

Books for children about the strength to overcome struggles and obstacles:

The Undefeatable by Kwame Alexander

Baseball Saved Us by Ken Mochizuki

The Wall by Eve Bunting

The Doctor with an Eye for Eyes: The Story of Patricia Bath by Julia Finley Mosca

After the Fall (How Humpty Dumpty Got Back Up) by Dan Santat

Emmanuel's Dream: The Story of Emmanuel Ofosu Yeboah by Laurie Ann Thompson

FAITH IN HUMAN SPIRIT

When my husband and I got married our Best Man, Bill was a great man; he was a loyal friend, a great coach and a wonderful teacher. He was so honest and forthright and you always knew where you stood with him. He believed in and always saw the best in his athletes, his students and his fellow man. He was also very handsome with a smile that genuinely touched your heart. One of my girls on my track team said, "Oh my, he is a slice of heaven!" He was close.

He was also a big prankster and would continue the tradition of what is known as "Hickman letters" letters originated with Tom Hickman, a teacher and coach. These letters were written on school district stationary to admonish behavior of a fellow staff member or principal, all of course with a fictitious signature and usually fictitious facts.

Tragically, Bill was 43 when he died due to Myocarditis, an infection of the heart. George spoke at his funeral about his passion for others, the love and concern for his special education students, his skill in coaching the throwing events and their special friendship. He talked of his love for sweets and how he would walk from his house to the local grocery store with a spoon in his pocket and finish off a half-gallon of ice cream on the way home. But mostly he talked about his faith in his fellow man, his ability to see the person and not the problem; his ability to celebrate small steps that led to big achievements. He made people better. After his death, a scholarship was created to honor his life and it is named Bill Degnan's Faith in Human Spirit Award. I think of him often, as I put a little piece of lint in a crock for him- something he did at his house just to annoy his wife. I remember how he was always kind, and how refreshing it was that he always had a genuine compliment for everyone as part of his greeting.

Bill used his voice to lift others up and had faith in human spirit.

Books on having faith in others:
Chicken Sunday by Patricia Polacco

Some Birthday! by Patricia Polacco

Gifts of the Heart by Patricia Polacco

PEACE

"Nonviolence is a powerful weapon. Indeed, it is a weapon unique in history, which cuts without wounding and ennobles the man who wields it." Dr. Martin Luther King, Jr. (38)

Today, I am watching George Floyd's family tell the country that they want PEACE and peaceful protesting and not looting, burning and destruction. They also want justice and change. His brother, Terrence's words encourage peaceful change, he says, "Let's stop thinking that our voice (es) don't matter and vote," he said. "Not just for the president, but vote for the preliminaries. Vote for everybody. Educate yourself. Don't wait for somebody else to tell you who's who. Educate yourself and know who you're voting for."

"Let's switch it up, y'all. Let's switch it up and do this peacefully, please," he said, adding for his brother, "I know he would not want y'all to be doing this." He then led a chant of "peace on the left, justice on the right." (39)

Let us heed Terrance Floyd's words and march peacefully, as we remember all the efforts of those who have worked so very visibly on the front line of justice that have been stopped by violence: Abraham Lincoln did not get to continue to build a better future of equality and justice. John F. Kennedy did not get to continue to build a better future of equality and justice. Martin Luther King, Jr. did get to continue to build a better future of equality and justice. Violence stopped them. Stop the violence and let us build a better future of equality and justice together.

As people protest for justice and equality, as people work together for a cure for Covid-19 remember

Henry Ford's words, "Coming together is a beginning, staying together is progress, and working together is success." (40)

We can do this, it will be hard, it will be messy and it will take time, but we can do this. Find your voice, find your cause, be proactive, take action and have faith in human spirit!

SMALL BITES

"Our greatest weakness lies in giving up. The most certain way to succeed is always to try one more time." Thomas Edison (41)

When I was little we had roller skates that you strapped on your shoes with clamps that fit around your shoe, to keep them on you used a key to tighten them. You always wore the key around your neck as a necklace, just in case the clamps loosened and you ended up with a skate hanging off your foot with the strap still wrapped around your ankle. Most of our friends had roller skates and we skated around our development and we also went to the skating rink. These skates had brakes on the toe, so we practiced stopping, turning and eventually skating backwards.

When our girls were in fourth and fifth grade, Rollerblades were popular, so we bought some and would skate around on our nice flat, smooth roads in our development. Now, Delaware is very flat, with very few hills except of course the Cape Henlopen State Park, or in northern Delaware. Cape Henlopen State Park, formerly Fort Miles, an Army Base during World War II, is hilly. The hills were created to hide the Bunkers and most were created as wind blew sand up against the Observation towers, trees and beach grasses. Over time walking and bike paths have been paved throughout the park. Well, someone had the great idea to rollerblade in the state park. Everything was going well, until we came to one of the big hills, it was tough going up, but going down was disastrous. Our girls were behind me and I was racing down so quickly, I decided to slow down and step off the path to wait for them. Gravity and my lack of practice stopping with my heels, led to a full speed face plant and slide into the sand. My lack of practice stopping on flat surfaces was magnified on the hill.

This is true about all learning, by practicing small parts or pieces of a skill in a safe environment, learners can master each part and build on those skills and eventually feel comfortable enough to take a risk, and bite off a bigger chunk of information to begin more learning or complete skills with less support and then independently. For me, it was just a small bite of sand and a little hurt pride!

Before the protesters go home, before the cities and stores are cleaned up and rebuilt, and just after we have taken a breath and collected our thoughts, we need to begin to tackle our conversations about the injustices we face as a country in small bites. We need to invite people from many different walks of life, government and faith leaders, the oppressed and the privileged, the poor and the famous, those who have used their platform and experiences to make a plea for change and unity.

This is the perfect time to ask ourselves tough questions. Am I biased towards people who are different from me? How can I challenge and understand my racism? What are my beliefs? Do my thoughts and actions reflect my beliefs? What feelings and actions have made me who I am? Am I who I want to be and what can I do to be a better, more accepting person?

We are ready for this conversation and ready for the work to begin. We all need to participate, maybe in small bites at first, but we need to participate and not give up. We can't be neutral.

"If you are neutral in situations of injustice, you have chosen the side of the oppressor. If an elephant has its foot on the tail of a mouse, and you say that you are neutral, the mouse will not appreciate your neutrality." Desmond Tutu (42)

Marvin Gaye's song "What's Going On? is a song about racial injustice, how too many people are dying and how if we talk, we can see and understand- what 's going on. His lyrics are succinct and powerful.

"What's Going On"(43)

Mother, mother

There's too many of you crying

Brother, brother, brother

There's far too many of you dying

You know we've got to find a way

To bring some lovin' here today - Ya

Father, father

We don't need to escalate

You see, war is not the answer

For only love can conquer hate

You know we've got to find a way

To bring some lovin' here today

Picket lines and picket signs

Don't punish me with brutality

Talk to me, so you can see

Oh, what's going on

What's going on

Yeah, what's going on

Ah, what's going on

In the meantime

Right on, baby

Right on

Right on

Mother, mother, everybody thinks we're wrong

Oh, but who are they to judge us

Simply because our hair is long

Oh, you know we've got to find a way

To bring some understanding here today

Oh

Picket lines and picket signs

Don't punish me with brutality

Talk to me

So you can see

What's going on

Yeah, what's going on

Tell me what's going on

I'll tell you what's going on - Uh

Right on baby

Right on baby

Books about being different:

The Mermaid's Purse by Patricia Polacco

Just Plain Fancy by Patricia Polacco

Mrs. Katz and Tush by Patricia Polacco

1 Confucius. (N.D.) quotes.net

2 Twain, Mark (N.D.) Quotable Quote goodread.com

3 AJMC, 2006,.

4 Kia's Accelerate the Good Program, 2020, YouTube.

5 Young, Ed. (2002) Penquinrandomhouse.com

6 10 Thought Provoking Lessons from Gandhi, 2012. Writechangegrow.com

7Did Albert Einstein says, "We can't solve problems with the same kind of thinking we used when we created them.2019,Https://wwquora.com

8 Biography.com Editors, 2020

9Juma, Norbert, 2020, #12 everydaypower.com

10History. Com Editors, 2020, July 6.

11Mitchel, Tia 2020 Ajc.com

12Atwell, Ashleigh Lakieva 2018 Blavity.com

13 Adams Noah, 2013, August 28 Nrp.org

14 Talk 2020, August 20 Wikipedia

15 History.Com Editors, 2009 October 27 History

16 Obsesses 2014, May 28 Glamour

17Scully, Kristina, 2020 Thepathway2success

18Kiger, Patrick J., 2020 History.com

19 Stowe, Harriet Beecher, 1852 ISBN 978-1508480129

20 Lincoln, Abraham, 1863, January 1 Archives.gov.

21Jefferson, Thomas, 1776, July 4 Archives.gov

22 Bleiberg, Larry, 2018 July 22.Latimes.com

23 McGarrity, Steven, 2020. Communitylegalaid.org.

24 Black Lives Matter Blacklivesmatter.com.

25Foston, Cheryl, 2013 Whatcherylersaid: wordpress.com

26Rodenhizer, Samuel, 2018 Quationcelebration.wordpress.com

27Little, Becky, 2018 History.com

28Blackpast, 2013 George Wallace Blackpast.com

29Cline-Ransome, Lesa 2020 The Power of Her Pen

30Ocasio-Cortez, Alexandria, 2020, Response to Ted Yoho's apology on the House Floor Youtube.com

31Khalid, Asma, 2020 Joe Biden and Kamala Harris make joint appearances on Npr.org.

32 Woodward, Avlin, 2020 Greta Thunberg Businessinsider.com

33Solly, Meilan, 2020 158 Resources To Understand Racism in America Smithsonianmag.com

34 Hakim, Joy, 2011 A History of US, KAA, Inc.

35Bryan, Ashley, 2016 Simonandschuster.com

36 Fitzgerald, F. Scott. Treasurequotes.com

37Carter, Jimmy and Rosalynn, 2020 Response to George Floyd's Death Cnn.com

38King, Martin Luther, Jr. (1964) MLK, wsu.edu

39Floyd, Terrance, 2020 Rev.com

40Brown, Joel, 2016 Addicted2 success Henry Ford quotes

41Edison, Thomas A.Brainyquote.com

42 Tutu, Desmond. Quotable quotes. Goodreads.com

43 Morey, Pete, 2019 cbc.ca Marvin Gaye

PART 2:

VALUES

CHARACTER

Someone once said, "Character is revealed when pressure is applied. We usually think that people with good character have traits or qualities like: honesty, loyalty, integrity, fairness, courage and that they make good choices. We also think that people with bad character traits are the opposite of the traits listed. In school, we talk a lot about character. We read books about honesty, loyalty, courage, hope, love and helpfulness that are integrated throughout our curriculum. We read biographies, nonfiction and fiction stories about these character traits and discuss them, write about them and talk about how we can or do exhibit these traits or qualities in everyday life.

We also know that it is easy to have integrity or be fair when things go well, it is easy to have courage when nothing is scary, and it is easy to be loyal when we feel loyalty from others. When times get hard, when we are scared or anxious, we have choices to make and our real character comes through, whether it is a good or bad character. During this difficult time or any trying time, your character is what your family and your children witness. How you react to a tough situation or trying times reveals your true character and children learn more from what we do than what we say. It is okay to be scared and sad, it is also okay that things are hard to handle and accept. It is okay that it is hard to always be patient and kind. I think the most important thing to do now or at any time that is difficult is to talk about your feelings with your family and yes, your children. It is okay for them to know you are having a hard time. When you talk about real life situations with your children, they will know it is always okay to talk about their feelings, their disappointments, their worries and their fears. It is important to tell children that you will listen to their fears and that you are there for them, but it is equally important that they know that sometimes you need to talk and sometimes things are scary for you, and sometimes things are not fair and you need them to listen. When we open up the lines of communication we allow our families to see and talk not only about our mistakes and difficulties, but also our victories or times when we can acknowledge and celebrate our good character and actions.

What does your character look like when pressure is applied?

Here are a few wonderful books for children that deal with character traits:

Dogger by Shirley Hughes and Strega Nona by Tomie DePaola are about Loyalty,

Amazing Grace by Mary Hoffman is about Fairness,

Pepito's Day by Luis Garay, The Empty Pot by Demi and Sam, Bangs and Moonshine by Evaline Ness are about Honesty

Wilfred Gordon McDonald Partridge by Mem Fox and Mama Do you Love Me? By Barbara M. Jossee are books about Love

Miss Tizzy by Libba Moore Gray, and Enemy Pie by Derek Munson are about Kindness

Fifty Cents and a Dream: Young Booker T. Washington by Jabari Asim and Bryan Collier is about hope

In Our Mother's House by Patricia Polacco is about diversity,

Stand Tall, Molly Lou Melon by Patty Lovell, is about self esteem,

<u>Trombone Shorty</u> by Troy Andrew and Bryan Collier and

<u>The Bracelet</u> by Yoshiko Uchida are about believing in yourself

OPTIMISM

"The pessimist sees difficulty in every opportunity. The optimist sees the opportunity in every difficulty." Winston Churchill (44)

During this time after you have taken care of your families, worked through lessons with your children, and maybe gone to work yourself, take some time to document your feelings and thoughts. My mother had a daily prayer journal that she kept most of her adult life. For me, prayer is optimism, looking for the good, praying for the grace to live life the best way you are able. Writing down your thoughts and feelings makes them concrete and allows you to evaluate these feelings. Are they hopeful? Are they optimistic? Why or why not?

We always have choices for every moment in our lives. We can choose to feel sorry for our situation and be stagnant and depressed or we can choose to be optimistic. Optimism helped make our country great, as people immigrated to our shores from other countries. These immigrants came with a dream, that here in a country, that fought for its freedom with teachers, shopkeepers, ministers and farmers as soldiers, anything is possible. Optimism spurred 6,000 African Americans to journey North during the Great Migration for the chance of a better, safer life with economic opportunities in industrial cities in the Northeast, Midwest and West. (45)

Optimism keeps protesters marching for social justice night after night; even tear gas, rubber bullets and arrests can't dim their hope.

Optimism is what Brayden Harrington had when he used the guidance and advice from Joe Biden, to help him better handle his stutter as he spoke. Optimism is what Brayden had when he made notes on his speech to help him navigate words that provided difficulty as he spoke to the audience of the 2020 Democratic Convention. (46)

Our daughter Rebecca is optimistic. She enjoys life and embraces experiences both simple and novel. Her laughter can be heard rooms away as she watches a funny show she has seen before. She energetically dedicates herself to each activity, from watching an ice hockey game, running on the beach at sunset or to planning unique techniques to use when tie-dying dresses. Her optimism is real, refreshing and makes my heart happy.

Optimism has also driven small businesses to open; optimism has allowed us to dream, to create and to build a strong future for our children. Optimism is what we need to have when we don't know what tomorrow will bring. Optimism is working together to solve great problems that we face as a people and a nation.

Optimism is contagious. Optimism leads to change.

"Optimism is the faith that leads to achievement. Nothing can be done without hope and confidence." — Helen Keller (47)

Books on optimism for children:

When Lightning Comes in a Jar by Ernest Polacco

The Junkyard Wonders by Patricia Polacco

Chicken Soup for the Soul: Think Positive for Kids: 101 Stories about Good Decisions, Self Esteem and Positive Thinking by Kevin Sorbo and Amy Newmark, and Stand Tall, Molly Lou Melon by Patty Lovell

FAITH

I was raised in a household that worshiped God and we attended services in a fairly progressive church for the time period. We had guitars and singers, we read the book, <u>The Cross and the Switchblade</u> by David Wilkerson as a church and discussed its meaning and application to life. We had covered dished suppers, Easter egg hunts, and variety shows; and each Sunday there was a call to ask Jesus into our hearts. Our church and our faith in God, was woven into all aspects of our lives and family activities. Our worship wasn't over the top, but it was genuine and real. My faith in God and Jesus has helped me throughout my life and guides most of my decisions and actions. As a person, who is at times sarcastic by nature, some of my decisions, words and actions have not been approved or sanctioned by God. I am still working on that!

Many things I did on my own, without thinking of the ramifications or how it may affect others, usually didn't turn out very well. We tend to learn more from our missteps than when things go smoothly. With my faith in God and my redemption from Jesus by His death on the cross; I can be forgiven and work to make better choices and live a better life by the grace of God.

Faith doesn't always have to be faith in God, or Christian faith. Faith can be as simple as hope for a better, safer future. We can have faith that we will work to do what is right and faith that others will try to do the right thing. We can believe that our leaders will lead with a calm, sensible plan of action that keeps us safe. We can have faith that we can create a future where we are better prepared to handle catastrophes, natural disasters, injustices and illnesses while protecting our most vulnerable.

Books About Faith for children:

The Radical Book for Kids: Exploring the Roots and Shoots of Faith by Champ Thorton

Everything Your Child Should Know About God by Kenneth N. Taylor

When God Made You by Matthew Paul Turner

If You Could Ask God Anything, Awesome Answers for Curious Kids by Kathryn Slattery

I AM, 40 Reasons to Trust God by Diane Stortz

The Storm That Stopped by Alison Mitchell

The Garden The Curtain and the Cross by Carl Laferton

The Prisoner and The Earthquake and the Midnight Song by Bob Hartman

Jesus and the Lion's Den by Alison Mitchell

Jesus Calling: 365 Devotions for Kids by Sarah Young

COOPERATION

As our world is battling Covid-19, I find myself thinking about the hot pads we used to make on a square loom when we were children. The loom had notches for each loop to attach to and then you would weave and secure the loop on the opposite notch. If you missed a notch or your notch was not secure, your hot pad would fall apart. To me this is an analogy that fits our current situation. We each have a loop to secure to the notch, but we also need to have everyone else secure their loop to the notch as well. To secure our notch we need to stay home, wear a mask and do our part to decrease the spread of the virus. We need to demand that all notches are secured to our collective hot pad by having adequate testing equipment for hospitals, adequate medical supplies and protective equipment for health-care workers and masks and safety measures in place to protect all who deal with the public. We need everyone to do their part. This ripple is far reaching and needs the help of our Governor, Senators and Representatives to ensure we are safe, adequately informed, protected and smart. We need to make sure that the hot pad we weave through our country is strong and secure enough to include all people in our towns, states and country and eventually we need to begin to weave that hot pad with the world, together in peace with a common goal of getting and keeping people safe and healthy.

I also know from history that through the pain of a plague, a war, or a natural disaster, good things happen. The Black Plague led to a sanitation system, and a system of building code to ensure houses were built safely. 911 brought more safety measures for air travel. War brought the Industrial Revolution and empowered women to productively join the workforce. The marches and protesting today for the murder of people of color may help us work toward equality and change, as racial inequalities are exposed by both the pandemic and unjust treatment.

To me our current situation of sheltering in place has already shown its silver lining, the fact that people are home together, playing games, reading books, working out, learning together, baking together and maybe making hot pads. This time, although it may be difficult, it is a gift to our family, a gift of cherished time together, time to learn more about our spouses, our children, and ourselves. This time away from others, will build stronger families, help us to have more empathy for others as events unfold, help us to find, and repair the flaws in our healthcare and educational systems, help us to recognize the need to help people who are not as fortunate as we are. In order for us to come out of this stronger, we need to be wiser and look at the systems we have in place and determine how we can change them, reinforce them and securely attach the loops to the notches.

As we weave a future that provides more equality, and more opportunities for people to better their lives, we all have a role in this, think about what you can do, what can your children do? God wants prayer, but He also wants action. We are in this together, how can we help?

Books on Cooperation for children:

Roxaboxen by Barbara Cooney

Ox Cart Man by Donald Hall

The Relatives Came by Cynthia Rylant

Mr. Putter and Tabby Series by Cynthia Rylant

Farmer Boy by Laura Ingalls Wilder

Pumpkin Soup: A Picture Book by Helen Cooper

The Magic Tree House Series by Mary Pope Osborne

ATTITUDE

IF YOU CAN'T CHANGE YOUR FATE,
CHANGE YOUR ATTITUDE (48)

Author and public speaker Bob Bitchin said, "Attitude is the difference between an ordeal and an adventure". (49) Yes, evidently that is his real name! But he is correct in knowing the importance of how our attitude during this time, or any challenging time, can make the challenge a painful ordeal or an adventure.

Currently, my Kindergarten students are completing school lessons using an online platform called Seesaw. We just finished learning about simple machines. I provided materials for many of our units in a "learning box" that were to be used as we read about each simple machine or other topics. During this unit, the students made different simple machines like a lever, wheel and axle, an inclined plane and then a catapult. Each student was asked to make a short video to share the simple machine they made. In each video that shared their simple machine, a sibling was usually present, actively and happily participating in the lesson. The most wonderful video came from a family with a homemade catapult on the kitchen counter, and the child was launching marshmallows into the mouths of alternative family members. This decision to make this an adventure instead of an ordeal has been the mantra of all my Kindergarten families, as they learn together and make memories they will never forget. I think by changing our attitudes and adapting to these new adventures, our experiences will positively impact how we look at and react to challenges and changes we may face in the future.

"Attitude is a little thing, that makes a big difference", Winston Churchill. (50)

Our attitude will make the difference as we endure this hardship. Will we be stuck at home with our children or will we be sheltering safely in place with our families?

EMPATHY

"EMPATHY IS…Seeing with the eyes of another,Listening with the ears of another,And feeling with the heart of another." Dr. Alfred Adler (51)

Empathy is the ability to understand another's pain as if it were your own, to learn from another person's experiences. In <u>To Kill a Mockingbird</u> by Harper Lee, a classic tale that echoes empathy on many levels, with a premise that to understand other people's thoughts and feelings you have to live in someone's else's skin and walk in their shoes. Empathy and morality are significant for life, and we can only truly appreciate and understand the people around us if we have empathy.

In the children's book <u>A Porcupine Named Fluffy</u> by Helen Lester, Fluffy finds empathy and understanding from a Rhinoceros named Hippo. If we can raise children who cannot only recognize another's pain, but act in a way that helps them feel better, we have done an amazing job and are on the way to create a better world for our future. Our empathy helps us look at the number of Covid-19 deaths displayed on our televisions each day to document our country and world's total, and realize that each of those numbers represents a father, mother, sister, brother, husband, wife or child instead of just a number.

Our empathy helps us look at protesters and try to understand their pain, and hear their voices and appreciate the urgency of their cries.

Empathy can be learned as it was in To Kill a Mockingbird or A Porcupine Named Fluffy. Children can learn empathy in various ways. Children are being taught to be empathetic, as they make cards or signs for healthcare workers, form a Go Fund me page to generate money for the masks they are making for others, as they make a rainbow of hearts to hang in their windows as a sign of hope and thanks to healthcare workers, as they make a stained glass chalk cross in their driveway, or help deliver meals and groceries to the elderly, or to not just stand to protest injustice, but learn about it. How can we show empathy?

Books on Empathy for children:

The Lemonade Club by Patricia Polacco

Charlotte's Web by E.B.White

The Trees of the Dancing Goats by Patricia Polacco

My Rotten Redheaded Older Brother by Patricia Polacco

Brave Irene by William Steig

Hey, Little Ant by Phillip M. Hoose

Elmer by David McKee

Something About Hensley by Patricia Polacco

Old Henry by Joan W. Blos

COMPASSION

"True compassion means not only feeling another's pain, but also being moved to help relieve it." Daniel Goleman (52)

A compassionate person is a person who is empathetic to others pain and suffering. I am passionate about books, and love how books are a perfect way to share inspiring stories and lessons of compassion. My favorite children's author and illustrator is Patricia Polacco. Her life has been filled with such wonderful, and sometimes painful events that shape her stories. Each of her glorious books weaves a wonderful tale filled with emotion, compassion, empathy, heartache and happiness. Her books allow children and adults to authentically experience the events of her book, make real life connections to these events and then they can talk about those events. Holes in the Sky (53) deals with Patricia's journey, as she tries to find her grandmother Bubba's sign to her that she is watching over her after she goes to Heaven. In this amazing story, Patricia finds her Bubba, not in holes in the sky, but in a loving person that she meets in the form of a new and compassionate friend.

I wholeheartedly love all of Patricia's books, but some of my very favorite are:

Welcome Comfort,

The Keeping Quilt,

The Blessing Cup,

Pink and Say,

The Christmas Tapestry

Mr. Lincoln's Way,

Chicken Sunday,

Mrs. Katz and Tush and

Rechenka's Eggs.

Sharing books allows families to share a special, nurturing time together to cuddle and enjoy an experience together, as books magically take us to another place and time and allow an escape.

Books teach us compassion, give us hope and help us to understand our feelings and can provide a springboard for discussions about compassion for others.

LOVE

"The best thing to hold onto is each other." Audrey Hepburn (54)

As a teacher in a Christian school, I talk a lot about love, as our mission is to teach children about God and Jesus' love for them and the sacrifice Jesus made for each of us by dying on the cross. Our main purpose as a school, besides education, is to learn about Jesus' love and help children want to ask Jesus' spirit into their hearts as their savior and teach them how to share this love with others.

Love can be defined in so many different ways, the love we feel for our parents and family, the love we feel for our children, the love we feel for our students and their families, the love we feel for our friends, the love we feel for the beauty in the world, the love we have for adventure, or exercise, the love we feel for our homes and yards or even love for a favorite food, like strawberries with meringue shells and vanilla ice cream. The amazing thing about love is that when you give love you get love back. The same thing is true about hate. When we hate and show hateful actions and share hateful messages, we get hate and generate hatefulness. Hate in our country is just as strong as the thread of love. For years it seems to have been hidden somewhere just below the surface. The freedom to express hate and derogatory, divisive comments and salacious words has quickly bubbled to the surface and exploded over many modes of communication, such as social media and the news. This hate is shrouded in written word without any face-to-face interaction, reaction or accountability. Strangers can comment in hateful ways to a post from a person they don't know and have never met. This impersonal method of opinion sharing or admonition is generally without consequences, remorse or understanding.

How do we respond to hate? How do we explain this hate to our children? How do we resolve the deep seeded, generational hate, and begin to heal the wounds of the past?

In schools, we respond to hate by teaching kindness. We discuss kindness and what it means to be kind. We reward kindness with praise and acknowledgement. We read books about kindness and write about kindness. We value kindness and are kind to all children. As parents and teachers, we can model kindness to all people, even the unkind. Our children learn more from our actions than our words and will follow our example. Though it is evident that kindness isn't enough on its own, to overcome generational hate and inequalities, it is a great beginning.

A wonderful book about generous love is <u>What is Given from the Heart</u> by Patricia C. McKissack (55). In the story when Otis' father died, he and his mother were suddenly very poor and quickly lost their farm. They moved into a run-down house and had very little. One Sunday, before Valentine's Day, their reverend at church told of a family whose house had burned down in a fire. He urged the congregation to find and give things to the family that might be useful. Otis' mother was quick to begin thinking of things she would want and need if they lost their house. Otis was hesitant. His mother made an apron out of her best tablecloth, telling Otis she was stitchin' this with a loving heart. Otis was still undecided. Finally, he used his paper and crayons and made a book about the little girl for his heartfelt contribution. When the girl received Otis' gift he had made, she was grateful and happy. As Otis and his mother walk home his mother expresses her joy about how their gifts had reached the hearts of the family. As they approach their house they notice a love box on their steps and their hearts rejoice!

When we were little we used to stand on the ottoman and sing into a hairbrush. The song, *Put a Little Love in Your Heart* (56) was frequently requested, so put a little love in your heart and when you give from your heart, our world will be a better place.

Think of your fellow man
Lend him a helping hand
Put a little love in your heart
You see it's getting late
Oh, please don't hesitate
Put a little love in your heart
And the world will be a better place
And the world will be a better place
For you and me
You just wait and see
Another day goes by
Still the children cry
Put a little love in your heart
If you want the world to know
We won't let hatred grow
Put a little love in your heart
And the world (And the world) will be a better place
All the world (And the world) will be a better place

For you (For you) and me (And me)

You just wait (Just wait) and see, wait and see

Take a good look around

And if you're looking down

Put a little love in your heart

I hope when you decide

Kindness will be your guide

Put a little...

Books on Love and Kindness for children:

Chester's Way by Kevin Henkes

My Sister Gracie by Gillian Johnson

Be Kind by Pat Miller Zietlow

The Red Bicycle: The Extraordinary Story of One Ordinary Bicycle by Jude Isabella

I Walk With Vanessa: A Story about a simple act of kindness Kerascoet

Ordinary Mary's Extraordinary Deed by Emily Pearson

The Giving Tree Shel Silverstein

How to Heal a Broken Wing by Bob Graham

The Story of Jumping Mouse by John Steptoe

Amos and Boris by William Steig

Do Unto Otters by Laurie Keller

Betty Doll by Patricia Polacco

The Wonderful Things You Will Be by Emily Winfield Martin

A Pocket Full of Kisses and The Kissing Hand both by Audrey Penn

COURAGE

"You cannot be afraid to speak up and speak out for what you believe. You have to have courage, raw courage." John Lewis (57)

When we talk about courage in school, we discuss things like: going upstairs by yourself when it is dark, or staying in your bed during a thunderstorm instead of running to your parent's room, and standing up for someone who is being mistreated, or just having the courage to do the right thing. We read books about being courageous, like Thundercake by Patricia Polacco or Brave Martha by Margot Apple, but the reality of courage is exemplified and personalized as we read about the early life of Ruby Bridges.

Ruby Bridges was six when she became the only black child to attend William Frantz Elementary School in New Orleans, Louisiana in 1960. After the passage of Brown versus The Board of Education in 1954, that determined that the segregation of schools was unconstitutional, the National Association for the Advancement of Colored People (NAACP) encouraged families to send their children to white schools. Ruby's parents agreed to send her to the all white school. With amazing courage, and protection from Federal Marshalls, she walked to school daily in a nice dress and a bow in her hair passing screaming, angry mobs that would terrify many. Each day she prayed two times for the angry mob, once on the way to school and again on her way home. Her prayer was simple, yet powerful. "Please God, try to forgive those people. Because even if they say those bad things, they don't know what they are doing." (58)

This type of courage has been exemplified in others throughout history as they stand up and do what is right despite the personal danger.

John Lewis' life is an example of living your faith and following your convictions, with optimism, and consistency. To fulfill what he felt was his moral obligation, he said, "The Civil Rights Movement was based on faith. Many of us who were participants in this movement, saw our involvement as an extension of our faith. We saw ourselves doing the work of the Almighty. Segregation and racial discrimination were not in keeping with our faith, so we had to do something." (59)

As a young man, John Lewis was moved by the message of Martin Luther King, Jr.'s speeches he heard on the radio and then became actively involved in the Civil Rights Movement. John Lewis led as he marched, organized demonstrations, gave speeches, was beaten, bloodied and arrested more than forty-five times as he fought for equality. In 1965, in Selma Alabama, he led the march for voting rights across the infamous Edmund Pettus Bridge, where police in battle gear met the marchers. Lewis was badly beaten and then hospitalized with a fractured skull. The march became known as "Bloody Sunday". (60)

John Lewis continued his fight against injustices as a Congressman until his death on July 17, 2020. His death comes in the midst of a renewed movement for social justice. He remained optimistic about the force of these protests and stated how these "new" protests not only gave him hope, but also should provide hope for us all. He continued to encourage peaceful marches and never wavered from his original intent to be a peaceful, moral leader.

As we are able to look back on his life and his incredible determination to fight inequality on all levels, we can be inspired by his words to get in the way and get in good trouble. Documentaries, books and articles on his legacy and his life will remind us how far we have come and encourage us to follow his path to move forward. His words and actions will inspire us to be resolved for change and keep working toward equal justice. He believed we all possess the courage to stand up and do the right thing, to make a difference, to make a more perfect union and create a better world.

With hope in his heart he acknowledged these words about our nation, "We have come a long way in America because of Martin Luther King, Jr. He led a disciplined, nonviolent revolution under the rule of law, a revolution of values, a revolution of ideas. We've come a long way, but still have a distance to go before all of our citizens embrace the idea of a truly interracial democracy, what I call Beloved Community, a nation at peace with itself." (61)

We have come a long way because of John Lewis. I think we can get into some "good trouble" and harness the courage to work toward change and rise up together. As you read the words of the song, *Rise Up* with lyrics by: Cassandra Monique Batie and Jennifer Decilveo, be inspired to rise up a thousand times again. We can no longer be silent, we can do the hard work together with hope and courage and....

Rise Up (62)

You're broken down and tired
Of living life on a merry go round
And you can't find the fighter
But I see it in you so we gonna walk it out

And move mountains

We gonna walk it out

And move mountains

And I'll rise up

I'll rise like the day

I'll rise up

I'll rise unafraid

I'll rise up

And I'll do it a thousand times again

And I'll rise up

High like the waves

I'll rise up

In spite of the ache

I'll rise up

And I'll do it a thousands times again

For you

For you

For you

For you

When the silence isn't quiet

And it feels like it's getting hard to breathe

And I know you feel like dying

But I promise we'll take the world to its feet

And move mountains

We'll take it to its feet

And move mountains

And I'll rise up

I'll rise like the day

I'll rise up

I'll rise unafraid

I'll rise up

And I'll do it a thousand times again

For you

For you

For you

For you

All we need, all we need is hope

And for that we have each other

And for that we have each other

We will rise

We will rise

We'll rise, oh oh

We'll rise

I'll rise up

Rise like the day

I'll rise up

In spite of the ache

I will rise a thousands times again

And we'll rise up

Rise like the waves

We'll rise up

In spite of the ache

We'll rise up

And we'll do it a thousands times again

For you oh oh oh oh oh
For you oh oh oh oh oh
For you oh oh oh oh oh
For you

RESPECT

"Respect yourself and others will respect you." Confucius (63)

When we are respectful of other people's opinions and ideas, even though they may be different than our ideas we exhibit tolerance and acceptance. At times it is difficult to be tolerant and respectful of others opinions and ideas when they are so divergent to our way of thinking. It is challenging, but it is vital that we work at it.

My mother had a phrase, I am not sure where it originated, but it was "Stick-to-a-tivity". She used this phrase when we needed to put more effort into something that was difficult to achieve. It was an encouraging phrase that sticks with me today when I find it hard to be respectful or to diligently work to understand the different opinions and ideas of others without judgment.

When talking about respect with children, we usually talk about people who earned respect from others, by overcoming a difficult situation or remaining calm and poised in the face of prejudice and mistreatment. This makes me think of Jackie Robinson and his journey as a young boy growing up in an all white neighborhood, to rising up to a second lieutenant in the Army, to be later court-martialed for his objections to racial injustices in the service and then his struggles as the first black athlete to play Major League Baseball in 1947. As Jackie answered Branch Richie's request to join an all white league, he was thrust into the spotlight of baseball's desegregation and quietly listened to taunts from teammates, spectators and umpires. He was spit on, and threatened but, athletically and skillfully played the game and excelled. When he had enough, he found his voice and stood up against the bad call, and the taunts, all while playing and working hard. He was named Rookie of the Year in 1947 and then MVP of the league in 1949 and led his team to the World Series six times and they finally won the championship in 1955. Through hard work, standing up for what was right and sheer determination, Robinson fought discrimination and racism and earned respect.

But think for a moment about the impact of Jackie joining a Major League Baseball League team in 1947 without an invitation? What would that have looked like?

The book Teammates (64) by Peter Goldenbock, chronicles the struggles he faced and how he overcame these obstacles and how this provided opportunities for all black athletes to play professional sports.

Jackie's Nine, Jackie Robinson's Values to Live By (65), written by Jackie's daughter Sharon Robinson, provides a unique and personal insight to his nine values that guided and strengthened his resolve as he fought for equality. The nine values Jackie lived by are: Courage, Determination, Teamwork, Persistence, Integrity, Citizenship, Justice, Commitment and Excellence. These values earn my respect.

Jackie Robinson said," *I'm not concerned with your liking or disliking me... All I ask is that you respect me as a human being."* (66)

We are raising and teaching a generation of children that will shape the future of our world. With love and respect, and when we add Jackie

Robinson's Nine Values and stick-to-a-tivity, we will have citizens who can achieve anything, face any problem, conquer any obstacles with equality and fairness.

GRATITUDE

When one door of happiness closes, another opens; but often
we look so long at the closed door that we do not see the one,
which has opened for us. — Alexander Graham Bell (67)

When I was young, times were a little tight financially. My grandmother wanted to make sure that my sisters, my brother and I never wanted for anything, so Christmas at her house was a sea of presents that covered both the dining room and living room floor. We got wonderful things, amazing books, toys, hand-knitted sweaters, clothing and sweet maple sugar candies. We were very grateful for her sweet generosity and thoughtfulness, and every gift was lovingly made or purchased for us and very much appreciated and enjoyed. We have all probably had privileges or things that we have been given by our parents or our grandparents that are extra things we enjoy, but are not necessities.

With these wonderful gifts and opportunities we feel gratitude or thankfulness. Sometimes we obtain too many things, our garage full of books, wreaths and bikes attests to that fact.

In school, we read a fantastic book, <u>The Quiltmaker's Gift</u> (68) by Jeff Brumbeau, about a King who is so greedy that he celebrates two birthdays a year to ensure he has everything he could possibly want. When he finds a Quiltmaker, who makes quilts for the poor, he wonders why he has never received one. The Quiltmaker tells him," My quilts are for the poor and the downtrodden", which he is neither. After many angry attempts by the king and his soldiers to make her sew him a quilt, she tells him to make gifts of everything he owns. Of course, he is resistant to do so, but when he finally begins to give away his things, he discovers happiness from his generosity. As he travels the world to give away his treasures a sparrow flies back to tell the Quiltmaker. Each time a sparrow lands, she sews another stitch in the quilt. Tired and poor he returns with a happy heart, and with one last present for the Quiltmaker, his throne. Then with surprise and gratitude he receives his beautiful quilt just as the Quiltmaker promised. The King is forever changed by this experience and now helps the Quiltmaker deliver quilts to the poor and the downtrodden.

For children to understand gratitude they need to understand generosity. Children need to think about things they are grateful for, things like a strength they have, something that makes them happy, something in nature that is inspiring, something they did that was hard to accomplish, something that is beautiful, something that is simple that we sometimes take for granted. Besides just recognizing gratitude and being grateful, children also need to work for things they want, complete a daily chore to earn some money and buy something they have been hoping for. Working towards a goal and then achieving it creates the feeling of gratitude for a job well done.

It is important to make gratitude part of your daily conversations with your family, maybe deliberately add this topic to your daily dinner conversation. Ask yourself what made you feel grateful today?

Here is a quote that resonates the gift of gratitude.

"Some people could be given an entire field of roses and only see the thorns in it. Others could be given a single weed and see the wildflower in it. Perception is the key component of gratitude. Gratitude is a key component of joy", Amy Weatherly. (69)

Our perception of our situation or our circumstance, will either help us deal with it with strength, hope and gratitude or our negative attitude will make it extremely difficult.

MINDFULNESS

The present moment is filled with joy and happiness. If you
are attentive, you will see it." Thich Nhat Hanh (70)

Imagine that you are fully engaged in a task, you are aware of your
thoughts and feelings, but not obsessed or controlled by them. You are
focused on the present, not worrying about the past or about the future.
Your attitude is positive, curious, and non-judgmental, that is mindfulness!
(71)

I know it is hard to be mindful and not panic or worry, when dealing
with an unknown future like we currently are dealing with or spending all
day with small children adjusting to a new schedule. It is important to be
mindful and present in activities with your children and family. It is also
helpful to you and beneficial for your children to have time apart. If you
have an infant, nap-time could be the time your older children play quietly in their rooms or watch a television show, while you take a moment
to stretch, rest, do yoga or just sit and have a cup of tea and breathe. This
is also a wonderful time to teach our children mindfulness. You can teach
your child to take deep breaths or count to ten, when they feel anxious or

unsettled, do yoga together, help them find a strategy that helps them to be aware of their feelings and identify them. As you identify your feelings with words, it will help your child identify the feelings they have also.

When our daughter, Rebecca was nineteen months old, Hannah was born. Someone told me to think of Hannah coming home to Rebecca, the same way I would feel if my husband brought home a new wife. Immediately, it was clear, though I would have appreciated the extra help, I was not interested in having this happen. I realized this could be a challenge to navigate as Rebecca got used to sharing us with Hannah.

I knew I had to be mindful of Rebecca's feelings, which was difficult since she was so young and spoke in her own language of long da da du da da du paragraphs. I needed to lessen her panic, and find a way for her to identify and understand her feelings. I drew pictures that depicted each feeling and added words, like jealous, happy, upset, sad, and worried, so I could help her to identify those feelings with words, then we could talk about them and I could help figure out how to help her. I made a poster with Velcro to attach the pictures and match them with the feelings, so she could bring me the picture of the feeling she had and we could talk about it. We also had a list of things she could pick from after she identified her feelings, instead of having a meltdown. The list included reading a book, going for a walk, sitting on my lap or playing with Hannah. Not long after we had mastered this feeling identification chart, her long wordless paragraphs turned into words and words and words.

This experience helped both of us use words to identify feelings and be mindful to how those feelings affect our actions and behaviors. She did test this relationship one day, as she was stroking Hannah's little hand and telling her, "I love you, sweet Hannah", and then bent over to bite her hand and looked at me and then gave her a sweet kiss. I am sure she was just keeping me on my toes!

Though you are busy, sometimes overwhelmingly busy, try to find time to be mindful of your feelings, and your actions, take a breath, sip some tea, listen to music, enjoy a good book or create art. To have time to be mindful, it helps to have a plan for your time. In order to have time to set aside for mindfulness, prepare things that you can the night before, clean as you go, plan your meals for the week or cook together on Sunday for the upcoming week. It helps to have a regular bedtime and routine for your children and do one load of laundry each day. I used to have everyone wear the same shade or color of clothing, so when it was bath time and shower time, I put the clothing in the washer and after we were finished with bath time and ready for books, I put the laundry into the dryer. After reading books, telling stories and prayers, I folded the laundry and put it away. This simple plan helped me to have more time to be mindful and present.

Books for Mindfulness for children:

I Can Do Hard Things: Mindful Affirmations for Kids by Gabi Garcia

I am Peace: A Book of Mindfulness by Susan Verde and Peter H. Reynolds

LAUGHTER

"Laughter is an instant vacation." Milton Berle (72)

We began watching The Marvelous Mrs. Maisel (73), a wonderfully filmed magically costumed hilarious show. It is laced with bad words, which I don't appreciate, since my bad words are usually shoot, darn and an occasional poop. Despite the bad words, it is funny. The characters are extraordinary, personable, real and so very uniquely funny as they tackle the stresses and problems of their lives. Laughter is always welcomed, and very healthy and now more than ever it has provided such a wonderful break from our harsh reality of 2020.

We all probably have a few things we say that only our family thinks are funny and those lines become our entertainment moments. When I was really young, I told my family that. "I liked preachers that cracked funny ones". When I was a little older and my mother began teaching, we were supposed to complete our daily chores and homework before she and my father got home My sisters and brother thought they could boss me around since I was the baby of the family and with my hands on my hips

I told them that, "I don't take orders from unauthorized posteriors." I still don't.

When I was in middle school, M*A*S*H (74) was a very popular show, we always made sure that we had eaten dinner, washed and put away the dishes and all homework was finished before it was time for it to start. I had a huge crush on Alan Alda's character, Hawkeye. I even had a scrapbook that I would cut out all the weekly descriptions of the show or any pictures that were in the newspaper and glue them in and add a date to the top. This crush was fueled by his humor, he was funny in the operating room, the mess hall, everywhere, I was smitten by laughter and then there was Tom Selleck!

One night on Jimmy Fallon (75), New York's Governor, Andrew Cuomo, was his remote guest. Fallon thanked him for his calm, honest, smart, and informative and science based handling of the novel Coronavirus and that it meant so much to him. He also reminded him that as a single man who has been the voice of reason and leadership, he had a new following of adoring women, that Jimmy labeled as "Cuomosexuals". Now, is that funny, or just inappropriate?

Our daughter Hannah is funny! She is quick witted, with one-liners that make us laugh and keep us laughing. She just has an amazing talent, to make anything funny. I discovered it is her follow up sentence that is the real key to her humor.

They say laughter is the best medicine and I believe that is true. How can you be worried or sad when you are laughing?

Books that are funny for children:
The Best Book with No Pictures by B.J. Novak

Where the Sidewalk Ends by Shel Silverstein

The Pigeon Needs A Bath! By Mo Willems

Click, Clack Moo, Cows That Type by Doreen Cronin

Nibbles, The Book Monster by Emma Yarlett

Stuck by Olover Jeffers

What George Forgot by Kathy Wolff

Dragons Love Tacos by Adam Rubin

The New LiBEARian by Alison Donald

The Gruffalo by Julia Donaldson

GRIT AND DETERMINATION

Grit can be defined as one's ability to set goals and work really hard to achieve them, and to keep working hard despite failures or setbacks. Grit can also be: determination, focus or the strength to keep working to get something completed. Gumption is a word we often heard at our house growing up. We needed gumption and focus to achieve something that was difficult for us. If you had gumption, you not only reached your goal, but you received praise for a job well done.

Rebecca and Hannah both have Grit. They are both amazing students and athletes and used grit and determination to achieve many goals. Both my husband and I were track athletes, we actually met at a coaches meeting he was hosting and we both understand and admire grit and determination.

As the girls were growing up, we would go over to track practice and they would run around the track with girls on his team. They also went with me to all the track meets, since I ran the finish line and scored the meet. We had a pop up tent that I would put next to the scoring table and in it were games, toys, a sleeping bag, snacks and drinks. Usually, one or more of the girls on the team would be in with them playing a game or reading a book to them between their events. They grew up at track meets and listening to us talk about effort, determination, setting goals, grit, success and winning and losing.

In Middle School, both girls played Field Hockey and ran for the track team and also participated in Hershey Track and Field Meets. They had grit, determination and were extremely competitive and successful. As they entered High School, they added Cross Country in the fall with Field Hockey and Rebecca added one year of Lacrosse to spring track. As athletes, who were also daughters of the coach, they were often moved to any event that got the necessary points for the win. Most of the time their events involved running from one end of the track to the other to take a jump and then run a race. Rebecca is a distance runner and also was a triple jumper, and usually the mile was just after the triple jump. If you don't know anything about track and field events these are direct opposite events and usually distance runners don't jump. In the triple jump you run down the runway at controlled top speed, hop as far as you can, then step as far as you can with the opposite foot and then jump as far as you can into the pit off your other foot. Any jumping event quickly fatigues your muscles as you pound on the hard runway. So imagine taking three triple jumps in a small meet or six in a big meet and not even having the chance to switch out of your sand filled shoes to your racing flats and get on the track and race a mile in under 5:20 or whatever it took to score the needed points. That is grit!

Hannah is also a gifted athlete and would triple jump, sprint, run middle distance races or any event the team needed her to compete in for a win. During her senior track season, she learned to hurdle and high jump, both very technical events, and did it well enough that she won the 300-meter hurdles and finished second in the high jump for our state track championship to ensure a state meet title for the team. At the beginning of her 300-meter hurdle race at the state meet, Hannah was not where she needed to be. She had a slow start, something that is almost impossible to overcome in a sprint and even more difficult when you add hurdles. But somehow, Hannah dug in and worked so hard, that she seemed to impossibly make up time over each hurdle and through sheer grit and determination won.

In college they both choose to play Field Hockey, at University of Delaware, a Division One school, in of course Delaware. Division One sports are tough and require grit and determination and participation takes a toll mentally and physically. At the end of Rebecca's freshman season, there was a coaching change.

This coaching change had both positive and negative effects on our girls, the coaching was elevated, but the pressure and intensity were extremely high. The new coach had moved from a big Division One school that was very successful and consistently in the NCAA sweet sixteen. His goals were to get Delaware to win the CAA tournament and get Delaware to the NCAA tournament within four years and win the National Championship within six years. These goals required quite the learning curve and tremendous pressure for the athletes.

The girls also ran indoor track for Delaware, a program that was competitive but more relaxed. This experience provided a nice change from the intensity of field hockey. With a lot of thought and discussion, Hannah made a tough decision to switch to Track and Field full time in the spring of her sophomore year and give up her Field Hockey scholarship. With grit and determination, hours of strenuous work and some coaching from her favorite coach, her dad, she became a very competitive Heptathlete, which is no easy task and also earned a track scholarship. She had to learn to throw the shot put, learn to race the short hurdles, and learn to throw the javelin and refine her long jump. The Heptathlon is seven events over a two-day period, with a time limit for each day. The first day, athletes run the 100-meter hurdles, throw the shot put, sprint 200 meters and then finish the day with the high jump. The next day is the long jump, the javelin and the 800-meter run. These events required diverse training, dedication, stamina, focus and skill. Each year her times and distances improved and she ended up second on the all time list of Heptathlon performances for the University of Delaware. Her effort and focus needed to accomplish this is an incredible example of both grit and determination.

Meanwhile, Rebecca was playing field hockey with injuries that made her leg either go completely numb or feel like they were being cut by shattered glass. She had surgeries for the tarsal tunnel, nerve decompression and compartment releases one leg at a time. At the time she lived in an apartment with no elevator, so she and Hannah checked into a hotel. Hannah took care of her during the night and I came up to drive her to class and she slept on Hannah's big bear in the car, and iced her leg in between classes. It was amazing how many lecture halls are not handicap accessible, but Rebecca navigated on crutches until the end of the semester and made it home to recover. She worked through each surgery and recovery valiantly and worked with grit and determination to come back and play. Since she missed the majority of games her junior year, and since she had an additional year of eligibility, she added another major. Early in her Super Senior season, she was hit in the head with a drive by a teammate and had a serious concussion that lasted for eight weeks. Finally, after many forms of treatments that were unsuccessful, she went to a sports chiropractor, whose treatment led to her recovery. She finished her season with a special concussion headband and me praying for her safety on the sidelines. That is grit and determination.

Books About Grit and Determination for children:

Thank you, Mr. Falker by Patricia Polacco

The Bee Tree by Patricia Polacco

The Art of Mrs. Chew by Patricia Polacco

RESILIENCE

Resiliency is when life knocks you down and you get back up. Sometimes, life is difficult and we experience terrible things. When we are optimistic and determined, we can overcome obstacles and become stronger and more resilient.

My husband has coached for 41 years. He has coached Cross Country and both Indoor and Outdoor Track and Field. In 2010, he had a physical and told the doctor he got a little tight feeling in his chest when he ran with the kids. As a precaution, he had a stress test where his results seemed fine. Around 5:30 the next morning, we got a call from the doctor to make sure he didn't go for a run. He needed a stent put in to open his blood vessels. Not long into this process, they determined that he needed a quadruple bypass. As the dedicated track coach he was, he wanted to schedule his surgery when it worked into the track schedule. So mid March, on a Friday he had surgery. He recovered well and set a daily goal to complete a certain number of laps around the Coronary Care Unit and worked hard to fulfill all the requirements he needed to be discharged from the hospital. By the following Tuesday, to everyone's astonishment, he was up in the press box announcing the results of the track meet. That is resilience and a little bit of crazy!

Last summer, while at Disney World, we got a call to tell us that George's biopsy was nodular malignant melanoma. Here we were with two days left of vacation at one of the hottest, sunniest places around. We knew the spot they took off was strange, and seemed to appear out of nowhere and was probably not good, but we were not prepared for that news. Shattered, we tried to act stoic and not show our worry to each other, while looking at all the "over tanned" people as we walked around Animal Kingdom and Epcot.

When we got back, we told our girls and had appointment after appointment, test after test. After determining that the melanoma had escaped and was in one of his lymph nodes, the best course of action seemed to be the removal of all his lymph nodes under his arm and to install a drainage pump. After a month of infections, he began to heal, while I constantly searched everywhere for information, and read book after book about melanoma. Seven books later, I found the best book that made sense and was informative and easy to read, Dr. William Li's Eat to Beat Disease The New Science of How Your Body Can Heal Itself. (76) The premise of this book is that food is medicine, and can boost your immune system, prevent and fight or starve disease and compliments regular medical treatments. Dr. Li, lists five foods you should eat daily to prevent and defeat cancer: Dark chocolate 85% cocoa or higher, Sourdough bread made with rye flour, Green tea, Kiwi and mushrooms including the stems.

He also lists juices to drink before x-rays, scans and cancer treatments, which are Guava, Watermelon, Grapefruit and Tomato Juice. I blend watermelon to make juice, and then blend all the juices together, except the tomato juice he drinks either before or after the juice mixture. I made charts of the five categories of food and the specific benefits from the back of the book: Angiogenesis- stop tumors from growing their own blood vessels, Regeneration- helps stem cells, Micro-biome- increase good gut bacteria, DNA Protection and Immunity. I also made a weekly chart, so I could make sure he eats foods from every category each day. The foods are all delicious and readily available. Dr. Li talks about how

Pomegranate juice restores your micro-biome and makes treatments for cancer more effective.

This process has been scary and hard to fathom, but the silver lining is that George is walking everyday, riding his bike, doing exercises, doing his breathing exercises, dry brushing to stimulate his lymphatic system and he uses a machine on his arm each day to help circulate lymphatic fluid. He is resilient, optimistic, determined, prayerful and thankful. We have had a set back this summer, and will continue on with prayerful optimism.

About five years ago, a teacher at our school was diagnosed with Multiple Myeloma (77), a cancer that forms in a type of white blood cell called a plasma cell. With this disease plasma cells that help you fight infections by making antibodies that recognize and attack germs become cancerous and multiply. This cancer causes cancer cells to accumulate in the bone marrow, where they crowd out healthy blood cells.

Despite my efforts to have her wear a mask or keep her distance from our children at school, she continued to hug them and come to school when she didn't feel well. Each year since her diagnosis, she has spent the whole school year sick with a cold or pneumonia. She began eating the five cancer fighting foods from Dr. Li's book, Eat to Beat Disease this past August and did not get pneumonia this school year, but did have a few mild colds. This diet was the only change she made in her health regimen and I believe it helped her be resilient to sickness.

Books on Resilience:
The Bravest Man in the World by Patricia Polacco,

Because by Mo Willems,

Mufaro's Beautiful Daughters by John Steptoe,

Yen Shen by Ai-Ling Louie,

The Rough Faced Girl by Rafe Martin,

<u>Stellaluna</u> by Janell Cannon

<u>Adelita</u> by Tomie dePaola and

<u>Unstoppable: How Jim Thorpe and the Carlisle Indian School Football Team Defeated Army</u> by Art Coulson

44Churchill, Winston Brainyquote.com

45Editors, History.com 2020, The Great Migration History.com

46 Weissert, Will, 2020 Apnews.com

47 Keller, Helen Brainyquote.com

48 Tan, Amy Goodreads.com

49 Bitchin, Bob, 2017 Soundingonline.com

50 Churchill, Winston, 2013 brainyquote.com

51 Adler. Alfred, goodreads

52 Goleman, Daniel, brainyquote

53 Polacco, Patricia, 2018 penquinrandomhouse.com

54 Bright Drops, Audrey Hepburn. Brightdrops.com

55 McKissack, Patricia C., 2019. Penguinrandomhouse.com

56 DeShannon, Jackie song en.winkipedia

57 Lewis, John. Goodreads.com

58 Coles, Robert, 2000 amazon.com The Story of Ruby Bridges

59 Lawton, Kim, 2004. John Lewis pbs.org

60 Klein, Christopher, 2020 Bloody Sunday. History.com

61 Lewis, John MLK Jr. quote azquotes

62 Day, Andrea, 2015 Album: Cheers to Fall En.wikipedia

63 Hutyra, Hannah Keepinspiringme.com

64 Goleenbock, Peter, 1992 Scholastic.com

65 Robinson, Sharon, 2001. Abebooks.com

66 Robinson, Jackie (n.d.) Quotetab.com

67 Sasson, Rema, When One Door Closes Another Door Opens, sucessconsciouness.com

68 Brumbeau, Jeff, 2001 Quiltmaker's Gift

69 Weatherly, Amy. Herviewfromhome.com

70 Hanh, Thich Nhat, treasurequotes.com

71 Williamson, Tina. 2018 Mindfulamxing.com

72 Berle, Milton Quotetab.com

73 Marvelous, Mrs. Maisel, (2017) en.wikipedia.org

74 M*A*S*H, (1972-1983) en.wikipedia.org

75 Bowker, Brittany (2020) Jimmy Fallon hosts Gov. Andrew Cuomo Bostonglobe.com

76 Li, William, MD (2019) dr.william.com

77 Multiple Myeloma, Mayo Clinic

Mayoclinic.org

PART 3:

THOUGHTS ON LEARNING

COMMUNITY OF LEARNERS

Community of Learners can be defined as groups of people who share values and beliefs and who actively engage in learning from one another. (78) To me, that sounds like a family. As educators, our methods for teaching and supporting students at school mirror the nurturing, engaging education parents provide for their children at home. In school, teachers want students to feel and be safe, to be comfortable enough to take risks, ask questions, expand their thinking, and develop a love for learning-all while trying their best.

To include insight to methods and practices teachers engage in as they teach, it would take hundreds of books. So I highlighted things teachers do in school that are helpful for broad learning at home.

Creating a Community of Learners in School

The most important concept for the first few days of school, for a teacher, is to set the expectations for learning and to convey the following thoughts to each student that: I am here to support you. I will create engaging, purposeful lessons to make learning exciting. I expect you to do your best, and I will hold you accountable for your learning. I will provide you with every possible opportunity I can, to help you learn. I will welcome all questions and will work to help you learn that mistakes are learning opportunities. As a teacher, I am here to help students be successful academically, socially and emotionally. I am here to teach, model and practice rules and routines that have logical consequences for misbehavior, so we can all learn in a safe environment. I am here to provide children who misbehave the opportunity to fix and learn from their misbehavior without humiliation. I am here to help children learn social and emotional skills that they need to be successful both in and out of school. Through our studies, our readings and our everyday activities, I will teach social behaviors such as, cooperation, responsibility, empathy, self-control and academic behaviors such as, stamina, determination, and perseverance. Together we work to create a community of learners who feel supported, respected and heard.

A great book that exemplifies the concept of a community of learners is, <u>One Hen: How One Small Loan Made a Big Difference</u> (79) by Katie Smith Millway. This book is based on the true life of Kwabena Darko (Kojo), who lived in a mud house in a small village in the Ashanti Region of Ghana and how he helped his community, his town and his country work together to create change and opportunities for a better life.

In the book, after his father's death, Kojo must quit school to help his mother gather firewood to sell. In this poor village, the residents promise to donate their extra money to create a pot of money for each family to borrow to use to purchase something that will help them make their lives better. With the money, one family buys two baskets of fruit to sell, one family buys a sewing machine to sew dresses and shirts to sell, Kojo's mother buys a cart to hold the firewood they sell and with the leftover money, Kojo buys a hen. Kojo takes good care of his hen and sells the eggs at the local market until he has enough money to buy another hen. Now Kojo and his mother have an egg to eat each morning. With the profits Kojo makes from selling eggs from his now 25 hens, he can pay his fees for school and return to continue his education. As Kojo learns more about farming and raising chickens, he begins to set goals for his future which includes continuing his study of farming in college. After he graduates his dreams take shape as he seeks to get a loan from the bank for $900.00 to buy more chickens and wire to make a fence. When he is denied the loan at the local branch, he goes to the head of the bank and tells his story about how he began a business with one hen and then is granted a loan. As his business grows, he hires more people who in turn begin to prosper. He then starts a trust to give out small loans to others who have dreams of beginning a business and can't get a loan from the bank. This successful entrepreneur story has inspired the creation of the organization, OneHen.org. (80), that provides teacher resources, curriculum and at-home projects to help and guide students as they work to create small businesses.

In our Kindergarten class, to help develop a community of learners and get to know each other, we use ME Bags (Pinterest). Children bring in a ME Bag that has five things that tell them about them. As we share things from each child's bag, we not only learn about each child, but we can see how we are different or how similar we are to each other. We may have the same hobby, like the same foods or toys. Sharing our ME Bags also allows us to practice giving compliments or to practice using an "I" statement for the person sharing their ME Bag." I" statements are: "I noticed that you had Lego blocks, you must be creative, or I noticed that you have a book, I also like to read".

We also read The Name Jar (81) by Yangsook Choi, a book about a girl named Unhei (Yoon-Hye) from Korea, who wants to change her name so American children will like her name and not make fun of it. A classmate has the idea that everyone can put names in a jar that they like for her and she can choose a new name. Her friend helps her realize that her name is beautiful and she decides to keep it. To compliment this book and strengthen our classroom community we learn more about each other as families share with us the story of how they choose their child's name. This activity shows how love, thought and significant meaning contributed to the process families used to choose the perfect name for their child.

To encourage a community of learners each day during our circle time; every child has an opportunity to share something that they are thinking about or experiencing or to share a meaningful life event. Then together, we read a pledge that provides a daily reminder of our academic and behavioral expectations and how we need to work together to support learning.

Last, we share our morning message that provides our focus for learning, provides a quick review of concepts or skills and asks a daily question to help prepare students to begin thinking about new information we will be learning that day and also designates the daily greeter to welcome fellow students.

Throughout the school year, we continue to develop our community of learners with many activities, but some memorable activities are part of our Immigration Unit. At the end of the school year we learn about immigration and its impact on our country and United States' history. Our country has both welcomed immigrants from around the world, and also disgracefully captured, sold and enslaved others. In both instances, customs and traditions from those countries have been blended together to make our country unique. For students to learn more about the heritage of their families and where they immigrated or originated from, we gather information from each family. For each family we paint a family tree, which includes family members including great grandparents. We make a coat of arms that includes all flags from all the countries each student's family has immigrated from. This coat of arms serves as an additional way for us to celebrate how we are a community of learners, as we observe how our families may have come from the same countries or a way to celebrate our differences and similarities. During this discovery time, we also learn a little bit about each country as we read from The Lonely Planet Kids Travel Book: A journey through every country in the world (82) by Lonely Planet Kids.

During our Immigration Unit we read informative books like:

The Story of the Statue of Liberty by Betsy and Giulio Maestro,

Her Right Foot by Dave Eggers,

Emma's Poem: The Voice of the Statue of Liberty by Linda Glaser, The Memory Coat by Elvira Woodruff,

The Keeping Quilt by Patricia Polacco and

Coming to America by Betsy Maestro.

Books we read on the first day of school to create a community of learners:

School's First Day of School by Adam Rex

This School Year will Be the Best by Kay Winters

Parent's role in developing a community of learners

Parents are a vital part of our community of learners. They are children's first teachers and are part of all learning from the day their child is born until-forever. Parents have the unique opportunity and privilege of encouraging children to use their minds: to think for themselves, to ask questions and be curious, and to constantly strive to learn more. Parents can provide amazing learning opportunities for their children through books, cooking, art, projects, games, travel and collaborative stories.

This year with our remote learning, we added parents and siblings to our community of learners in a different way. They were there to help, encourage, explain and participate in the learning. One day I had a Zoom time that someone did not show up for, so I asked one of my Kindergarten children to join me for the time and her mother ended up talking with me. I wished I had the insight to set up Zoom times with parents to tell them how well they are doing with remote learning, or to see if I could help them or just to talk. We will work on that for the upcoming school year.

Community of Learners on television

NBC has a show called Songland (83). The premise of the show is to provide an opportunity for four songwriters to pitch their original song to a famous singer or group. The show is hosted by Grammy nominated Ester Dean, 4 time Grammy winner Ryan Tedder from OneRepublic and Shane McAnally, a Grammy winner with 40 number one records. All are also songwriters, singers and producers. As they listen to the songs, they dance in their seats, and share encouraging smiles! They immediately collaborate ways to make the song better, they add new rhythms, another guitar chord and "tweak" the melody; they change a few words, or make a stronger hook. The guest artist then chooses three of the four songs to be reworked and refined to better fit their style. After the collaboration, the artist chooses their favorite out of the three songs to record. This is an amazing example of a community of learners. The process that we witness in this songwriting collaboration is what teaching and learning is all about. They share ideas, offer support, rewrite, practice singing the song, work on it again and again, until they have the best possible song they can write and record.

After the one lucky song is chosen they are all sincerely happy for one another, both collaborators and writers. We have to remember as teachers and parents that it is the process of learning that is so vital and if the process is solid, supported and well planned with appropriate sized chunks of learning material, learning is successful.

Another wonderful show that models the concept of a community of learners is *The Village* (84), named for the apartment complex where groups of people live. All the people in the apartment complex are dedicated to the welfare and wellbeing of each other, and have become family. The show chronicles the life of Sarah and her daughter Katie, and their complicated and intertwined relationships with the people of the village as the show reveals their struggles and strengths. This amazing show unfortunately, was not renewed for a second season, but it's message and intent is vital for us to learn from. Imagine what we could accomplish if our world worked together as a village to care for, help and support each other?

We need to embrace our community and learn from each other. We need to learn how to support each other respectfully and always look for the best in each other.

POSITIVE BEHAVIOR MODIFICATION

Think back and remember that child that you may have seen lying on the floor having a fit at the grocery store because they couldn't get what they wanted? Everyone has experienced this, either as a spectator, a parent or as the child having the fit. When this happens, it is difficult for everybody to know what to do to be helpful. It is tricky! When you find yourself in this situation, take a breath and remember you are not the first or the last parent that will face this behavior either publicly or privately. But there are some steps to help mitigate or reduce these situations before they happen that may help.

I think the first step is to remove labeling, think of the child as not strong willed or naughty, but independent and determined; both of these qualities are very beneficial for life.

The second step is to understand that clear, consistent age appropriate rules give children behavior parameters to follow. (Usually the same number of rules for the age of the child) The rule: Make Good Choices is an all inclusive, effective rule.

The third step is to really listen to your child and talk to them respectfully. Notice, acknowledge and reward the moments when they make good choices independently. We all internalize specific praise and it can motivate and modify behavior.

The fourth step is teaching your child how to calm themselves down by: Counting to ten, taking deep breaths, walking away or telling a friend or parent how they feel or any strategy that you and your child decide on.

The fifth step is offering controlled choices to allow a child to have a say and to be involved in the decision making process, as well as having input to find a solution.

The sixth step is to help your child communicate their feelings clearly and learn to resolve conflicts.

The final step is to help them be socially aware of other people's feelings, to be empathetic towards others and appreciate diversity and different opinions.

Reading books together provides an opportunity for discussion about realistic choices characters have to make as they solve a problem in the book. You could ask your child what they think of the behavior the character displayed, or if the character made a good choice? What would they do in that particular situation? How do you think the character felt? Why? What do you think happened that made the character feel that way? I wonder how that would feel?

By setting up the expectations for situations before they happen, you can prepare your children and increase the odds that you will all have a fun, tantrum less trip. Before you go to the grocery store, make a list together of things your child can help you get, add things they can pick out, like cereal, the type of apples they like, their favorite flavor of ice cream.

As you shop you can give them choices like: "This or that?" "How many? ", "How should we do it?" The key is to offer a limited number of choices that you agree with, and offering choices prevents negotiation that will help avoid a power struggle, and always avoid choices that aren't available. These little choices help children feel like they have a say in what is happening. If you remind them as you go along of your expectations and add genuine and specific praise, you could turn a potential combative experience into a great adventure. Everyone loves specific praise, "I like how you are getting those oranges and putting them carefully in the bag, it looks like you are picking the sweet, tasty ones." "Thank you for your help today, it makes shopping fun to have you as my helper."

"We did it, we got everything we needed, was there something you were hoping to get, that wasn't on our list?"

It is also important to be firm about expected and acceptable behavior, for purchases before you enter the store, expectations for exiting a social situation and expectations for interacting with others. When we establish boundaries with clear, consistent rules that both keep our children safe and teach them that we don't always get what we want, we help set them up for success. If we provide the structure children need and the information about why we have rules in place they may push back less.

When our girls were little, they each had cute Bear backpacks filled with small games, magnetic tic-tac-toe, magnetic builders, crayons and paper, books and Polly Pockets for restaurants. We talked, played " I spy " games, the ABC game, where you find something that begins with each letter of the alphabet in order and often used the backpack activities to play together as we waited for a table or for our food. All these activities helped us teach appropriate expectations for behavior in a restaurant and gave them the opportunity to choose the activity they wanted.

We also went to our local library for story time. The librarian would read a great selection of books and then put those books out on the table for people to check out. Well, this could create a problem, since there were more children than books. So to prevent unhappy girls, I would remind them that Mrs. Miller was going to read some great books and share them with us to take home. We may not get the book you want, since there are so many friends at story time. So, I would ask, " What do you think we should do if we don't get a book?" or, "What can we do if someone else gets the book we were hoping to get?" We talked about our choices and which choices made the most sense. These proactive strategies helped our girls cope with the disappointment they felt when they didn't get the book they wanted to take home and also helped them understand the behavioral expectations I had for them.

If your child becomes that child lying on the floor kicking and screaming and cannot be calmed down in a public place, take them to the car. Help them calm down and tell them when they are ready to settle down and listen, we can talk about how you are feeling and what made you feel like you didn't have a choice. Tell them it is okay to be angry, but we need to work to figure out a way to solve this. Ask them, "How can I help?" or "What can I do to help you before this happens?" Tell them, "I am here for you no matter what." and "I will always help you figure things out." or "I am ready to listen, whenever you are ready to talk."

When dealing with a child who is aggressive towards another child or sibling, you do have to intervene with a hug to control the offensive body part. You need to say," I am stopping you from hurting …… until you can stop yourself." When they are calmed down and you have an opportunity to talk about how they are feeling, what do they think caused the problem, how can we solve it, how can I help you solve the problem. If they are part of the decision making process to find a solution, you are giving them the power to help themselves and to get more control of the situation.

By providing great choices for your child, you are helping them be in control of some situations: "Would you like mom or dad to read you a story?" "Would you like to walk slowly or quickly to the library? "Would you like this outfit or this one?", " Water with ice or lemon?".

If children are to practice making good decisions, it is important and helpful for them to make small choices when they are younger, since choices tend to become more difficult and more impactful as we grow older. By learning in schools and participating on sports teams with children with different expectations, it may provide opportunities for children to practice making good choices. Do they use the word they heard on the playground? Do they stand up for a child being bullied, do they use their voice to say no, and are they polite and kind to everyone? Do they go along with a crowd even if they disagree with the activity? These small decisions help your child put the values and expectations you have been teaching them and showing them into practice. These small decisions prepare them to make good choices later when the choices may become more difficult. We all like having choices and making (good) choices does give us power!

It is also important to allow children opportunities to make good choices on their own. When I was little, I had just lost a tooth and with the money from the Tooth Fairy, my sister and I walked to the store at the end of our road for a sweet treat. As we walked pulling our wagon and talking, I noticed a white butterfly flying around the wagon. I was convinced the butterfly was the Tooth Fairy reminding me to do the right thing and not buy candy. I can't recall if my mother reminded me to shop wisely before we left for the store, but I did know her expectations for my purchase. I did the right thing and listened to the Tooth Fairy butterfly, I bought a notepad.

When children have clear expectations established for behavior, they are very likely to do the right thing, even when no one is watching.

It is important that children have an opportunity to be part of the solution to problems their behavior creates to better understand the impact this behavior has on others and to develop strategies to resolve the problem to help make things right. When my husband was growing up, his parents implemented appropriate consequences that also became learning opportunities. If he or his siblings accidentally broke a window with a golf ball or baseball, they helped clean up the mess, replace the glass and then paint the window. Appropriate consequences reinforce the idea that mistakes happen and it is okay. By choosing to use mistakes or inappropriate behavior as learning opportunities we allow children to not only assume responsibility for their actions, but also to be part of the solution.

It is very important to have behavioral expectations taught and followed in school to ensure we have created an environment that is conducive for effective learning. In school, we use a class thermometer, which is a hand drawn thermometer with evenly spaced horizontal lines. For each segment, we decide together the things the children would like to earn for their good behavior. We earn: Pajama Day, Stuffed Animal Day, Dress Up Day and more. The all time favorite day to earn is Super Hero Day, and homemade costumes are always encouraged. These techniques to motivate positive behavior are most effective when children have a hand in deciding what they earn. During the school day, we add lines for both individual and class behavior as we work toward our new goal and celebrate great behavior.

Over the years, as a teacher, I have had some children with challenging behaviors. I think the most important strategy in dealing with challenging behaviors is to get to know the child, learn about the things they like, really listen to them as they talk, and stay as calm as possible and not get involved emotionally during the challenging behavior.

It is also important to be proactive and teach and practice expectations for behavior, and reward appropriate behavior, with specific and genuine praise, a high five or anything that seems effective, then react to inappropriate behavior. If you can identify what triggers the challenging behavior or what happened immediately before the behavior, this is extremely helpful. I had a girl in my class recently, whose behavior was both challenging and a mystery. It took me the good part of the first month of school to figure out what triggered her behavior. She would be fine and then swing quickly into a wild, crying fit, and didn't have the language to tell me what was happening or the coping skills to calm herself down. I finally discovered that transitions were difficult and that if I reminded her that we would be transitioning to a new activity in about five minutes, she was pleasant and had the time she needed to get ready for the new activity. Just this simple prompt calmed her and helped us establish a better way to communicate. This also helped me teach her calming strategies while she was calm, so she could use them when and if she needed them. We worked on taking breaths, counting, blowing on her hand and looking to me to give her a countdown from ten with my fingers as she took breaths. We still had moments of meltdowns, that were difficult, but by discovering that she needed a prompt to get ready for a transition was almost a miracle.

I have had other children with behaviors that escalated so quickly that it was hard to calm them down and the reasons for these escalations were not easily identified. I had a boy who was very bright and just was not confident at anything that required fine motor skills and really didn't want to try. His anger and frustration turned on more quickly than a light switch and escalated as quickly as a volcanic eruption. Our class that year required many creative behavior interventions and his behaviors were just not getting any better. I will always regret that I couldn't find an effective way to help him identify and control his feelings and actions.

By helping children identify their feelings and the feelings of others, they will be more likely to be able to identify if someone is happy, annoyed, upset, or uncomfortable and build relationships with others, while understanding more about their own feelings. Emotional

Intelligence is vital in social situations and life, and some people naturally can identify emotions, while others need help in identifying their emotions and feelings and using opportunities to self regulate their behavior.

If we can control and understand our emotions, we can better control our actions. If we can control our actions, we can guide our path. If we can guide our path, we can guide our future.

Schools and families need to support children with social and emotional learning opportunities. Games, books and conversations are wonderful ways to help children learn about and deal with their feelings and emotions and help them identify the origin of those feelings.

If you think your child needs more support or more effective interventions, it is important to contact a physiologist or a counselor. These professionals will provide your family with the help you and your child might need.

Early intervention is always beneficial.

Games to help develop social skills:
What Should I Do? Players face real life dilemmas and learn and understand the appropriate actions and consequences.

Didax Social Skills: 6 Board Games to help children develop coping skills, manners and identify emotions.

Teachers Pay Teachers (85), a collaborative site for teachers to sell games and activities for all ages and topics, provides a great array of games to teach social skills, manners, coping strategies and emotional health in both school and home settings.

Children's Books About Feelings and Behaviors:
When Sophie Gets Angry, Really, Really Angry by Molly Bang

I Was So Mad by Mercer Mayer

In My Heart: A Book of Feelings by Jo Witek

The Summer My Father Was Ten by Pat Brisson

Hands Are Not For Hitting by Martine Agassi PhD and Maricka Heinlen

B is for Breathe: The ABCs of Coping with Fussy and Frustrating Feelings By Dr. Melissa Munro Boyd

Listen Buddy, My First and Hurty Feelings all by Helen Lester

Wemberly Worried by Kevin Henkes

What if? In a Jar Questions and Dilemmas to Get Kids Thinking About Choices

By Free Spirit Press

Invisible Boy by Trudy Ludwig

The Recess Queen by Alexis O'Neill

The Color Monster by Anna Lienas

A Weekend with Wendell by Kevin Henkes

Spinky Sulks by William Steig

Babushka's Doll by Patricia Polacco

Julius Baby of the World by Kevin Henkes

The Bad Seed by John Jory

THE CHOICE TO FORGIVE

"There is no love without forgiveness and there is no
forgiveness without love." Bryant H. McGill (86)

Forgiveness is a powerful word that should be accompanied with powerful and real feelings. At times, it is difficult to teach children to ask for forgiveness with real emotion, as we expect or encourage them to say the words," I apologize", or "I'm sorry" after they have hurt someone or hurt someone's feelings. At the moment of the event, they may not feel remorse and the apology may be hollow and forced. The process of having children ask for forgiveness needs to be accompanied by the reasons we ask for forgiveness and those reasons need to be explained before, during and after a hurtful incident. We ask for forgiveness to mend a physical or emotional wound, but we need to understand why we need to ask for forgiveness or forgive another person. We need children to understand the power of their words, words that ask for forgiveness are powerful, but the words that accept the apology and add how it made them feel and that they don't want this to happen again are also powerful. People need options about how they receive and accept an apology. They can say, "Thank you, please don't do that again, it hurt me or my feelings." they can say, " I don't like it when you…"and not just accept an apology. Words are powerful and asking and receiving forgiveness is a great way to use the power of your words well.

A wonderful book that will forever change my life is <u>The Choice; Embrace the Possible</u> (87), written by Edith Eva Eger, a survivor of the Holocaust. She chronicles her life and her choices in three stages: her childhood before her internment, her determination for survival during her internment, and then her life during her journey after her liberation, as she unravels, digests and tries to understand her experience in Auschwitz. As a physiologist, she uses her unfathomable and painful experiences to help her patients recognize how the power of each choice we make can change our perceptions and our lives. Through this process, she herself begins to heal. For Edith, her freedom finally became real as she made the choice to travel back to Auschwitz to forgive her captors.

In Kindergarten, we talk about choices people have made throughout history: the choice to march peacefully for civil rights, the choice to sit for equality, the choice to stand up for those without a voice, the choice to work hard to overcome struggles and persevere with hope and faith. In school, we talk about how our thoughts, our words and especially our actions make us who we are and who we will become and how we need to make good choices and how at times, good choices take courage.

Books About Forgiveness:
<u>Matthew and Tilly</u> by Rebecca C. Jones

<u>Chrysanthemum</u> by Kevin Henkes

<u>The Friend Who Forgives</u> by Dan Dewitt

TRAINING THE MIND TO THINK

Albert Einstein said, "Education is not the learning of facts,
it's rather the training of the mind to think."(88)

My husband is currently having fun cooking most of our meals and is a chef in training, as he is learning new recipes, techniques and how the addition of spices we have never used really enhances the flavor. Who knew that by adding shallots, garlic and lemon zest could elevate the taste of green beans to incredible heights?

We have four meals a week delivered from a service that provides the ingredients needed along with a beautiful, detailed recipe card. As we were talking about how delicious the meals have been, he said he is just following a recipe and shared how it is amazing how chefs know what spices enhance the flavors of food and combinations or foods that compliment each other. I reminded him that as a chef learns to cook and bake, they begin by following a recipe and as they become more adept, and more skilled, they branch out and create new recipes and develop new combinations of scrumptious dishes.

As teachers, we continuously adapt our teaching methods and teaching strategies. We refine and differentiate those strategies to help find effective methods that ensure each student learns. The teaching community in general has always been great about sharing information and supporting each other to strengthen the educational process.

Teachers informally discuss helpful solutions to challenging learning styles, behavior challenges or a great strategy that worked well to help students learn. Teachers also meet formally to discuss solutions to problems as they arise, how to make instruction more effective or just to discuss something they have learned or to listen to an inspirational speaker. I think all vocations do the same thing to become more effective through discussions, practice, trial and error, mistakes, and then make adaptations and adjustments to refine their skill and effectiveness.

Not all classroom learning can be discussions, or child driven learning, and not all learning is fun. With everything we learn some of it is rote learning. We memorize letters and sounds through games, activities and books. We memorize numbers and then learn and understand the concept of a number. We learn and memorize phonemes, we practice them as we make words and then find them to help decode a longer word. All learning helps to train our mind to think, learn, and make connections to what we know and what we are learning and to expand our thinking to accept new ideas and views. Learning allows us to blend these new ideas with our own ideas, to challenge or refute traditional ideas or thoughts and to think outside the box to prove or disprove a theory or idea. When students are allowed to share their thoughts and ideas in a safe learning environment we create thinkers. Thinkers, who can challenge ideas, argue their point and listen and appreciate another person's point of view.

Accountable Talk (89)

Accountable talk is a model of intentional open-ended conversations that uses phrases and sentence stems, to help children be thinkers and convey and share their thoughts in a discussion in a thoughtful manner. Accountable talk helps students listen and add their comments, to ask questions, to clarify information and to stimulate a deeper level of thinking and learning. Accountable talk includes words and phrases like, " I agree with you because... but I disagree with you because..." "I wonder ..." "I like how you... " "Have you thought about...?", "When you said... I didn't understand what you were thinking, could you give me more information or explain it differently? " Have you thought about...?

This model provides a great foundation for students to have a voice in an environment that feels safe and provides support for those who are shy or reluctant to speak out and share information. Discussions and clarification of information helps students think deeper about a subject or to think on a higher level. This type of conversation is great for literature circles for children reading the same book, or for discussions about views and thoughts on historical and current events.

My husband is a retired teacher who taught Special Education for 37 years in our local public school. When he retired, I convinced him to teach with me four mornings a week. He promised me one year and we are now completing year number five. I must be pretty persuasive! It is easy to teach together, since we compliment each other in the classroom, both with our approach and common philosophies. We work together well, and sometimes model Accountable talk and our "out loud" thinking process as we teach our students. This process was very helpful to model for students as we complete lessons on Zoom. Everything about remote learning and teaching is new to us and to our students, so it is nice to think out loud and share how we are thinking and how we can clarify or expand on our thoughts or train our brain for thinking.

Each year in our Kindergarten class, after we study the Earth, we study Dinosaurs. Included in that study are the three periods of the Mesozoic Era: The Triassic Period, Jurassic Period and the Cretaceous Period. We talk about how the continents began as Pangaea or a Supercontinent in the beginning of the Triassic Period and broke apart into two pieces during the Jurassic Period and were more like today during the last period of the Dinosaur time, the Cretaceous Period. We talk about the climate, plants, weather and the types of dinosaurs from each period. We discuss topics like: Why do you think dinosaurs were small during the Triassic Period? Why were Masuria thought to be good mothers? What theory do you believe led to the extinction of Dinosaurs from Earth? These discussions provide great practice in Accountable talk, expressing opinions, expressing disagreement or agreement to another's view or opinion.

This type of interactive exchange can happen at your dining room table each night. You could begin with a topic that a family member is interested in and has read about and then discuss it. The daily news provides a wealth of topics to discuss and express an opinion on. You could read a chapter of a book together each night and retell the chapter and then discuss it, share views, make predictions, connections or share an opinion or what was learned. The History channel and website have amazing factual information on every possible topic. Watching and discussing these videos or reading the passages are also wonderful for learning, and for expressing opinions, sharing your point of view and listening to another person's point of view.

Accountable talk allows everyone to be part of the conversation in a productive way. The guidelines for accountable talk are non aggressive and provide a safe way to express feelings, thoughts and ideas, as well as challenge the thoughts and ideas of others. Accountable talk gives us a model to not just negotiate, but to think and expand our thinking by hearing and experiencing the thinking of others.

RISKS

"You have to take risks. We will only understand the miracle of life fully when we allow the unexpected to happen." Paulo Coelho (90)

In education and athletics, we take risks. We take risks when we share our opinions or answer questions. We take risks as we compete as an athlete, do I pass now and hope to hold onto my lead, do I run more conservatively and hang tight to the leader and surge past everyone at the end?

When I was little the freckles on my arms embarrassed me, so I would always wear long sleeves shirts to school. By nature, I am shy and didn't like to raise my hand in class. I was the model student, quiet, attentive and compliant. I learned, but never took risks. I never questioned much of the information that I was learning until my eighth grade spring. My gym teacher created a track club, an additional period of gym that gave us a chance to run, race and compete. For me, this was where I learned to take risks. I was fast and won race after race, somehow this confidence carried over to the classroom and I started to ask questions and contribute to discussions.

This confidence continued to permeate my life and helped as I continued to compete in high school and college and continues to help me now. I know that the confidence I gained as an athlete helped me to be more confident and more willing to take risks.

As a teacher, I encourage students to be risk takers. We talk about their responsibility to be active participants in learning. Educators use words that often reflect or label a concept that good teachers have always been doing or a new concept or idea that will help teachers become more effective. It is very important that vocabulary changes to fit the current situation, and helps everyone understand the concept. A fantastic example of this is Dr. Carol Dweck's Growth Mindset (91), a concept of believing that a "fixed mindset" assumes that we have a limited ability to learn and grow based on intelligence, but with a "growth mindset", your ability to learn is unlimited and that we learn from our mistakes, by working hard, trying again with a different method and that the process and effort are more important than the outcome. My philosophy and my approach to teaching and learning follows this model, but what I appreciate about the Growth Mindset model is that it adds an image of a gray brain and a colorful brain and words that talk about what good learners or growing learners do. Of course, we want the colorful brain, the brain that is active, thinking, connecting synapses, growing and learning. We do not want the gray brain that is dull and inactive. The concept of pictures and words is brilliant and very effective. I have a picture of a half gray and half colorful brain near our workshop area.

I have taken the words that describe a gray brain and the action required to create a colorful brain and laminated it and attached Velcro, so I can easily switch the encouraging strategies to working towards a colorful, thinking, growing brain. This addition of the gray brain versus the colorful brain image provides a perfect way for children to understand how their effort can impact their ability to learn.

Our daughter, Hannah is an elementary school teacher who works tirelessly to create a welcoming, creative environment for her students to learn. She is innovative, and always works to make connections to students and make learning fun. She has always had the ability to notice when someone needs help or extra support. When she was in Kindergarten, she would ride the bus to my school and help me with my afternoon class for four-year old children. Hannah had a knack for knowing when a child needed extra support and was always immediately ready to help them.

Today, in her classroom to help the children learn and understand that it is okay to make mistakes, she will make a mistake on purpose and have them help her correct the mistake. They talk about how making a mistake is okay, even expected and she will say, "Am I still cool? " "The students respond with. "You're still cool." This simple exchange reinforces that it is okay to make mistakes and we learn from them.

We need to own our mistakes and begin the hard process of fixing them with action that will make a change. If we do, that would be cool!

Books about never giving up and taking risks:
The Water Princess by Susan Verde and Georgie Bradiel,

The Boy Who Harnessed the Wind by William Kamkwamba and Bryan Mealer,

Salt in His Shoes by Michael Jordan,

The Book of Mistakes by Corinna Luyken

Giraffes Can't Dance by Giles Andreae

Flight School by Lita Judge

When Sophie Thinks She Can't by Molly Bang

Jabari Jumps by Gaia Cornwall

Hana Hashimoto, Sixth Violin by Chieri Uegaka

EXPECTATIONS

Expectations: a strong belief that someone will or should achieve something. I think we all have expectations for our lives, these may begin when we are little and evolve and change, as we get older. Our expectations for our lives are usually founded in our abilities, our interests and our experiences. My mother was also a teacher, and each summer we would always help her get ready for the new school year. I knew as we made bulletin boards, and wrote names on name-tags, organized closets and set up and rearranged desks, that I wanted to be a teacher too. I wasn't sure why I thought I wanted to be a teacher. Maybe I wanted to be a teacher because it was a familiar experience and, after all I spent a lot of time in school.

I really loved my first grade teacher Mrs. Leach. I don't remember everything about first grade, but I do remember the feeling I had in her classroom. I was the child that would hide in the car to go to the hospital with my brother when he got bitten by a dog when I was supposed to be at home or the one who would go shopping with my mother instead of staying home to play. I loved being with my mother and maybe that is why I loved Mrs. Leach. She was motherly, sweet and very kind. Her classroom felt safe, the expectation was to do your best as she gently guided us all to learn new things.

When my dog had puppies, our whole class walked to my house to see the puppies and I held Mrs. Leach's hand and led the way. I can't recall why exactly we visited our puppies, maybe we were learning about animals and their life cycles, but it might have been just for an exciting and memorable trip for our class.

As a teacher, I have always wanted my classroom to feel like a cozy place to learn. I have always had plants and a comfortable reading chair, nice bright learning rugs and a welcoming homey feeling. I have also always set high expectations for learning for each child. I believe that if lessons and materials for learning are well planned, if information is prepared in small bites and taught well, children can learn anything!

Everyone has expectations for their lives, how they hope their academic and athletic careers play out, expectations for their college experience and expectations for future experiences evolve and change over time. As we move through our life experiences, we meet people that may change our trajectory, or shift our focus and we may be set off course by new experiences and expectations. All these experiences and expectations are part of who we are and lead us to whom we become. My husband was married before and one tragic day his wife and Jenni's mother was killed in a car accident. The joys of this marriage and then the tragedy of her death shaped him. The past experiences both amazing and tragic are written on his heart and those experiences made him who he is, and who I fell in love with. Just as Jenni's love for her mother, along with the tragedy of her death and the memories she holds in her heart, have shaped who she has become.

The plans that we make are usually easily erasable, changeable and contain a rewritable blueprint. We need to remember that the process of these experiences is just as important as the product, the game, the degree, or the marriage. We need to value each experience good or bad and appreciate the lesson learned.

Many expectations and experiences are not positive. Both my sister and brother worked for many years as Social Workers who counseled welfare recipients. Over time, both of them became very jaded and disillusioned with the system. I am not sure if they couldn't implement programs that empowered and trained recipients for jobs, or saw something in human nature that discouraged them. The variable in our experience depends on people we interact with, their reaction, experience and impact on us. Many agencies dedicated to helping people can get bogged down, muddled and derailed from their original purpose.

Now, we have an opportunity to reset our expectations on how we treat other people, how we reach out and provide assistance to those in need and how we can fix the underlying problems that many programs have ignored or lost sight of, that they were created to address.

In President Barack Obama's virtual graduation speech to the class of 2020, he said, "You chose to become leaders and this happens to be a time when that's what we need most. If the world is going to get better, it's going to be up to you... It's your world now." (92)

We all need to have expectations for a better world and it can begin with the expectations we have to make changes, the expectations for our recent graduates and our own children. Each person has the responsibility to set the bar higher to help those in need to make sure our actions meet our expectations. Expectations help determine success.

EXPOSURE

As parents, caregivers and teachers we have the responsibility to expose our children to learning each day. These activities can be as simple as making a salad, measuring ingredients for a cake or building with cups or blocks or as complex as understanding the solar system, discussing a complex mathematical theory or learning a language together.

Some of our families are taking this time to learn together about a country every few weeks. They read books about the history and people of the country, prepare food to share and make traditional crafts, to learn and appreciate another country's history, culture and traditions. Others are making masks together to donate to those who need them, some are playing board games together and some are rollerblading.

This is the perfect time to have your children help you measure out the area for a garden, measure the perimeter to determine the amount of material you need to make a small fence around your garden, measure the area and plan out how to space your plants evenly. You can even start plants inside and transplant them when they have established roots. I planted potatoes in one of my planters and they are doing well. All you need is one potato eye, or just let them sprout and wait for them to grow. I also planted the bottom part of my lettuce and celery. The lettuce is doing well, but the celery needs more encouragement.

Playing board games provides a wonderful opportunity for families to spend time and is a springboard for all types of learning. At our house, we have a game cabinet, with games that have evolved and changed over the years. A few of our favorite games are: Addition 24, Subtraction 24, Multiplication 24, Mad Gab, Catch Phrase, In a Pickle, That's It, Think 'N Sync, Splurt and Reverse Charades.

Reading books together is always an impactful way to learn. Books provide endless possibilities for learning and are easy to obtain from a local library or a local bookstore.

You and your family could begin researching and planning your next vacation, you can read about the state or country together. Map out your travel plans, make a daily agenda, and plan where you would like to eat, shop and play.

Take advantage of every chance to learn and experience adventures together, they might be virtual experiences now, but preparing for future adventures can be an amazing family opportunity.

OPPORTUNITY

"The world is all gates, all opportunities, strings of tensions waiting to be struck." Ralph Waldo Emerson (93)

Opportunity is a situation or chance to do something. We all know that when we have an opportunity to try our hand at something new, we become better at that task with practice. When we learn to ride a bike, we have to fall, get up and try again, until we finally figure out that we have to be confident enough to pedal faster and keep our bodies balanced. Of course, we also need to practice stopping. The more opportunities we have to ride our bike, the better we will get at riding a bike.

With any type of learning, we need the opportunity or chance to try something new and then the opportunity to practice the skill until we master it, or at least get better.

When I was growing up we traveled by car or camper wherever we went, we never flew in an airplane until we visited our grandparents in Florida. We went as either the redheaded or blond grandchildren, and flew by ourselves under the careful watch of an airline stewardess, as they were called at that time. I just had the realization that we must have traveled as blonds or redheads due to the fairness of our skins and the strength of the Florida sun and how it would affect our outside time. What forethought, my grandmother had. Anyway, my immediate family always traveled by car, we sat with legs sticking to the hot seats, looking out the windows for cars from different states, or letters on signs to race to complete the alphabet first. We sang songs, slept, read and played games. One game was to see who could add up the numbers on license plates first, though my dad always won. We also stopped at all the little museums and interesting historical sights along the way. We had a cooler filled with lunchmeat and cheese, bread, mayonnaise and fruit. We had lunch stops at rest stops along the way and lots of bathroom stops for my sister. Traveling this way was an adventure and we had fun, it gave us an opportunity to be away from everything, to enjoy each other's company most of the time and then see how quickly my mother could reach back and inaccurately spank a leg if we misbehaved. We could "unstick" ourselves quickly from the seat and move our legs out of the way, while holding back our laughter. Since laughter may mean another attempt at a spank. Occasional spanks, hot legs, and this travel time together gave us opportunities and experiences we will never forget.

As parents, we have strived to provide our girls with all types of opportunities to experience new things like: music class when they were babies and toddlers, dance when they were in Kindergarten and first grade, gymnastics and art classes in second and third grade and horseback riding in middle school. These experiences were for enjoyment, to learn to move, to have fun dancing or tumbling, and they were opportunities to discover more about what they loved, and to decide if they wanted to continue with the activity or move on to something new. We scheduled these activities over a span of time so we weren't sacrificing one activity to fit in another. We wanted them to enjoy what they were doing and expected them to stick with it until the end of the class or session.

As Rebecca and Hannah got older they began running and competing in track meets and playing Field Hockey, we traveled a lot! Field Hockey provided many wonderful opportunities to travel, work with a team out of state and compete in tournaments all over the East and West coasts. We jumped at opportunities to travel to England, Holland, Belgium, and then to Argentina, and Uruguay, not just for the Field Hockey experience, but to discover different countries and cultures. All our trips were amazing opportunities for all of us. We had time with other parents to sight see, time with all the girls to enjoy scheduled trips and museums and time together as a family. These trips, though financially tricky, were important investments in our family.

Opportunities you provide for your children shape who they are and how they view the world. We have happily enjoyed many opportunities as a family to share experiences both big and small. We have coached our girls, cheered them from the sidelines as they competed both in track and field hockey, encouraged and helped them with school work, experienced and celebrated happy times and consoled them when things were hard. We have enjoyed each of these opportunities.

Our family has been blessed and enjoyed many opportunities to travel as a family, but trips don't have to be international to be memorable. The important factor is the family interaction, the family adventure. A family adventure can be a biking trip at a local park, a trip to one of our country's National Parks, a skiing trip, spending the day at the beach, going to museums and art galleries or camping in your backyard. The important part is the exposure to an experience and the opportunity to share it with family members. Currently, museums all over the world are offering virtual tours free. What an incredible opportunity to visit the Louvre and see Leonardo da Vinci's Mona Lisa with your family or watch a Broadway show in your living room, in your pajamas. The Getty Museum is asking people to recreate famous artworks with household items and post on social media to encourage creativeness and inspiration during this time at home. (94)

This challenge has provided a variety of amazing recreations of famous artwork. This is just another example of an opportunity to be present, to be creative and take advantage of something simple that will make a lasting memory.

Providing opportunities for people doesn't have to be large or a grand gesture, it can be in small acts of kindness that allow someone to have an opportunity they enjoy or learn from. My first teaching job was at a very small school and each year the whole school paraded down Main Street in Halloween costumes. My small class of children did not have costumes. We talked about what we could do to make costumes and happily I remembered that my brother in-law had given me this magical, pliable, stiff, paper-like fabric that we could use. Each child chose a favorite character from a book or a movie. We made hats, and masks, dresses and capes, we measured and sewed, we colored and painted and we had the most creative costumes in the parade.

This was a small opportunity we took together that I cherish.

Our daughter Jenni has always been a talented artist and has loved to make and create things since she was little. After graduation from the University of Delaware, she took an opportunity to head to New York to work in Graphic Design, doing work in print design and creative branding. As Graphic Design jobs were downsizing, she began her own company called PepperSprouts (95) and worked to build this into a successful company. She then created another company The Chatty Press, a Design Co. (96), which is a boutique stationery shop that creates custom Save the Date, Wedding Invitations, seating charts, menus, guest books and anything she and the couple collaboratively decide on. During this time when weddings are put on hold due to the Covid-19, she is making T-shirts to support peaceful protesters that say *Silence is Betrayal*, with all profits going to the National Bail Fund Network (97), which uses community bail funds as part of efforts to change local bail systems and reduce incarceration for both criminal and immigration cases. Jenni used time when she wasn't busy with her business to use her creativity and talent to help others.

Opportunity is not always fair and I feel somewhat embarrassed about the opportunities we have had as I look back on them, when others do not have the opportunity to feel safe in their homes and neighborhoods. In light of the protests that are occurring each day as a response to George Floyd's death, I feel like the media's coverage is more personal, more comprehensive and provided us with an opportunity to experience another's life. Growing up we just watched the evening news, which was a quick summary of world events and events happening in our country. Now, we have social media, people with cameras filming events and news is broadcast live, from city to city. Technology has allowed us to have the opportunity to listen as reporters talk with a group of people to allow them to weigh in with their opinions, thoughts and feelings. Witnessing these events is surreal and raw, as we can almost experience the events and feel emotions we usually would not feel, and experience things we usually would not see, as this coverage provides eye opening, real time assaults on humanity. Our country can no longer be indifferent to the tragic treatment of others due to the color of their skin; we need action that will lead to real and significant change. George Floyd's death leaves an indelible image on my mind and heart.

A photograph and words are blazed on my heart, of a Chicago woman crying in the car during peaceful marches to protest the unjust death of George Floyd by police, holding her smiling baby telling him,

"Look, Matthew, this is for you — this is so people can understand that you are not a threat when you're walking down the street." (98) This mother is hopeful that this tragic event and the protests for change will provide a better opportunity for her sweet son

Books on opportunity:

What Do You Do With a Chance? By Kobi Yamada

Ruby's Wish Shirin Yim Bridge

What Do You Do with an Idea? By Kobi Yamada

THOUGHTS ON TEACHING YOUR
CHILDREN AND SUPPORTING
THEIR LEARNING

When thinking about my years as a teacher and parent, I've concluded that learning revolves around these three components: Exposure, Expectations and Opportunity.

I also believe that school learning, while it has many social, emotional and educational benefits, is a very small piece of the learning puzzle; and that our exposure to great books, museums, travel, family learning experiences, talking, experimenting and participation in music, art, drama, athletics and competition are equally as valuable as typical school learning. The expectations family, teachers and community members establish for behavior, learning and actions, with support and instruction, will determine how well we interact with others, perform academically and help determine the success of the path you choose for life. High expectations, voiced or unvoiced, either from internal or from external sources, are powerful motivators to put forth the best effort, to be responsible for learning and improving, which leads to success. The opportunities to practice skills, both academic and athletic improve abilities.

Here are some amazing statistics from a Scholastic study that amplify how exposure to reading and the opportunity to practice reading skills and read books leads to improvement of these skills and dictates future learning success. (99) Children who are read to everyday, become readers.

Children who read for 20 minutes each day will be exposed to 1.8 million words per year and score in the 90th percentile on standardized tests.

A child who reads 5 minutes a day, will be exposed to 282,000 words per year and score in the 50th percentile on standardized tests.

A child who reads 1 minute a day, will be exposed to 8,000 words per year and score in the 10th percentile on standardized tests.

We need to expect children to read, and read or be read to everyday. When we read to our children, by supporting their reading efforts and being readers ourselves we show them the value of reading. We need to treasure books, and set the expectation that children read and provide opportunities for children to be readers and dreamers.

To help instill the love of learning and the love of reading, we read to our girls every night until the end of middle school. We often read the books they were reading in high school and college for a family learning connection. Reading is power and that power is available to all people, through public libraries, book boxes set up in yards and online read-aloud books.

Just imagine what your family could learn together if you varied the books you read, if you have learning themes and varied the topics and had literary circles to discuss books together.

Here are some steps to prepare children for reading, listening and understanding books better:

Before reading a book with children we want to talk about what they already know about the topic. We want to take a look at the pictures and the cover and make predictions about what the story may be about. We want to talk about vocabulary that may be new and unfamiliar and help the children come up with a definition that makes sense to them. We want to ask what are you curious to learn from this book?

During reading we want to ask children questions to keep them engaged, "What do you think will happen next? What does this remind you of? Does it remind you of a moment in your life? Does it remind you of another book you have read? How can the problem in the story be solved? What would you do and why? How do you think the characters were feeling?

After reading, we want to discuss the events and how they unfolded during the story. What was the problem? How did the characters work to solve the problem? Did you like the story? What was your favorite part? Would you change the ending? If so, how? What did you learn? Does this remind you of another book we have read or an experience you had? Would you recommend this book to a friend? Why is this topic important? How did the book make you feel? What is the author's message?

EXPOSURE TO INFORMATION

When we think about exposure to information as it relates to school learning, we want to provide students with opportunities to learn about a broad range of subjects and concepts. Currently, education in elementary school tends to focus on reading and math with little emphasis on history and science. Imagine if you are not adept at reading or have difficulty understanding mathematical concepts. With this narrow focus for instruction, we may diminish some students' interest in learning. We need to be reminded that we can teach reading strategies and skills effectively by using nonfiction books about animals, history, biographies, the world, athletics and more. Scholastic Company offers current event magazines from preschool to high school. With specialized editions in Art, Science, History and Cross-Curriculum topics, Language Arts, Reading Intervention, Math, and an issue called The New York Times Upfront that provide amazing learning opportunities. (100)

Instruction in science provides an opportunity for students to make predictions, experiment, gather information and record results. Science units emphasize hands-on learning and opportunities to work collaboratively with a group, develop critical thinking skills, form opinions and judgments that are supported by gathered evidence. Science in School, The European Journal for Science Teachers (101) online learning website, provides articles, information and even step by step directions for experiments on many different scientific topics. This format is an incredible resource for teachers and families, especially as children learn remotely.

Often, the learning of history in elementary school is narrowly focused on holidays, community, and occupations and almost never provides an opportunity to completely understand historical events. A comprehensive study of our country's accurate and chronological history can be planned, adapted and taught at each learning level. This would ensure that all students have a more complete understanding of history and the impact historical events have had on our country, the treatment of people, our laws and government and our educational systems. We can't expect children to have empathy and compassion for others, if their view and perception of the world lacks historical references of struggles and oppression of others. Nor can we expect them to celebrate the brave people who courageously faced and overcame adversity without historical references like these few examples: the soldiers who gave their lives for our freedom, the people who committed treason to write and sign the Declaration of Independence to make us a free nation, the Navajo Code Talkers who created an unbreakable code to protect the operations of the marines during World War II and learn from the scientist who kept working to find a cure for an incurable disease, or learn from the people who were told no, but accomplished great things. Like the Hidden Figures of NASA, Mary Jackson, Katherine Johnson and Dorothy Vaughn (102), the women calculators who did the math to ensure the safe landing on the moon and the math that brought them safely back to Earth.

We also can't expect children to understand the struggles and inequality others live, if our schools and communities remain segregated by historic zoning laws that were created and continue to be kept in place to protect and ensure property values in typically white neighborhoods remain high. Many elementary and middle school enrollments reflect the population of the community. Generally, public high schools are more integrated and more reflective of our world population allowing for a broader more accurate representation of diversity.

EXPECTATIONS FOR LEARNING

People are motivated to do well for many different reasons, expectations from parents and teachers, or expectations they have for themselves. Some people have an intrinsic ability to motivate themselves, set goals and work to reach them. But this is not true of all learners.

As teachers we have the ability to help set the expectations we have for student's learning. By explicitly teaching expectations for behavior with clear and consistent rules, teaching routes to travel within the classroom, teaching routines and schedules, as well as, specific activities that students can work on after they have completed an activity, teachers can set expectations for successful learning. As a teacher, I encourage my learners to take advantage of every opportunity they have to learn. I will help them learn by reading books, sharing information, by supporting their learning, but they are also responsible for their learning.

Many times during the day, we say, "Good listeners are good learners". We also talk a lot about what makes a good learner. What do good learners do? We make a list together and it usually mirrors my list. My list includes: To listen and then ask yourself if you understand what we are talking about? If not, what questions do you have to help clarify the information? To ask yourself, " how does what I am learning relate to what I already know, what connections can I make?" "Do I understand the directions?" " Can I restate the directions? " and finally, "Can I retell the information in my own words?"

OPPORTUNITY FOR LEARNING

My responsibility as a teacher is to be creative and present information and activities in a way that engages my students with interesting topics and allows all students an opportunity to learn.

When teachers include topics with a connection to a real life experience it helps learning to be exciting and, especially effective when students help guide the topics of study or can provide input to the material they are learning.

A vital step for teachers is to make sure students are learning and understanding what you are teaching. As we build on the information students are learning; we need to make sure they understand and learn each concept, so that they can retell the information and make a connection to what they know and what we are learning.

Each day as we learn about a country or topic, we spend time reviewing what we have already learned. We may use a poster or a chart we have made together to review information. Students can also take turns sharing what they have learned. This review process provides an informal way for me to assess children's understanding of what we are learning and provide them with positive feedback. It also provides a great summary of information, as well as feedback to me on whether or not I was able to help students understand the necessary information.

Like everyone, learners want feedback. How am I doing? Where do I need help? What can I do to improve? During our circle time, the student who is the teacher's assistant chooses the warm-up activity for our class. These activities are quick math games, or reading activities. These activities provide a way for students to receive immediate feedback from a friend or from me. Another important way to provide effective feedback is to have children help you correct or explain their process in solving a math problem or to clarify their writing. After lunch the students read me words from their word list or a book from a collection of books that compliment our learning themes. This provides a way for me to informally assess each student and provide effective, specific and helpful feedback.

It is also important to provide students with a variety of instructional methods. Children need the opportunity to work independently, work with a small group or a whole group. They need the opportunity to read a book, practice their fluency and comprehension independently or complete a variety of activities with some support, or be given a choice of how they investigate learning materials. Our local school district is currently using a reading series that has three research components throughout the school year and children get to choose their topic of study within those designated units. This method allows children to choose a topic that they are interested in learning about and may ignite a passion for more knowledge.

OPPORTUNITY FOR EXPLORATION

Math manipulatives, like pattern blocks, pentominoes, geoboards, and tangrams provide great opportunities for creative thinking and problem solving. Students love to make AB, ABC, and AABB patterns with pattern blocks. We practice patterns with our bodies like; hop, skip, hop, skip and more complicated patterns. Patterns are important in math as we learn to count by twos, fives and tens.

We use circle time to develop a concept of numbers; by having students hold up a certain number of fingers, when I ask, "Can you show me or 4 or 5?" We want students to understand that five is always five and when we make a larger number, we don't need to count out the first five each time. We can simply hold up one hand as five and then count up 2 more fingers as 6,7 to show the number 7. We continue with simple addition problems, by tapping the big number and counting up the small number on our fingers. An example is 5+3 = ___. We tap and say,"5", then count up three more as we say, 6, 7, 8", to answer the number sentence. We also play games with dice and a game called Compare, which is similar to War. We play Double Compare where we add up two cards and the person with the higher number gets all four cards.

During our circle time we also keep track of the number of days we have been in school in our place- value pockets with straws and bundle up the straws as we get a group of tens and then bundle ten tens to make one hundred. We keep track of the days of school on our Hundreds Charts, we keep track on a magnetic board with tally marks, with magnetic money, base ten blocks and on a ten frame. On our ten-frame mat we use yellow dots to correspond with the number of days in school and circle the even numbered dots. We have blue for fives and red for tens, so we can count by twos, fives, and tens and eventually count by fours.

We teach Fractions early in the school year, since understanding fractions help children better understand the concept of money and time. Everyday we complete a daily math page together. Each page has just five problems that may include addition, subtraction, money, fractions, time and a word problem. We solve these problems together and talk about the strategy we will use to solve each problem. We use our fingers, we draw pictures, use Touchpoints, dice, a hundreds chart and number lines. After Christmas, students will choose a problem to read or explain to the class and then they will decide the method we will use to solve the problem. Then they take us through the steps involved in solving the problem. This provides a great way to understand each child's thinking process as they solve math problems, but also helps them understand the strategy for solving the problem better. Often I will ask, "Did anyone use a different strategy to solve this problem?" It is important that students realize that there is usually more than one way to solve the problem and find the correct answer.

Some books to use when teaching math concepts:
Benny's Pennies by Pat Brisson

Jelly Beans for Sale by Bruce McMillian

The Coin Counting Book by Rozznne Lanczak Williams

Bunny Money by Rosemary Wells

Look at Annette by Marion Walter

Symmetry by Loreen Leedy

Domino Addition by Lynette Long

Actual Size by Steve Jenkins

Cook A Doodle Do by Janet Stevens

Inch by Inch by Leo Lionni

Just a Little Bit by Ann Thompson

Who Sank the Boat? By Pamela Allen

Eating Fractions by Bruce McMillian

What Time is it Mr. Crocodile? By Judy Sierra

A Second is A Hiccup by Hazel

Hutchins

A Second, A Minute, a Week with Days in it: A Book about time by Brian P. Cleary and many more.

EXPOSURE, EXPECTATIONS
AND OPPORTUNITY

Our daughter, Rebecca is a middle school art teacher, who designed her curriculum guided with her expertise from her Art, Art History and History degrees. Her curriculum exemplifies exposure, expectations and opportunity. She provides students with knowledge about famous artists through reading amazing books and Scholastic ART magazines. (103) She creates a five minute museum for her students, where they read primary or secondary source documents and discuss an article with topics like: Visual analysis-what do you see and what do you notice in the artwork? Vocabulary- that explains how the artist used line or an element of art or a principle of design in the artwork.

Her curriculum offers a variety of mediums and open ended projects in a choice based system, where students can choose not only their focus for their project, but the medium and direction they would like to go with their artwork. Rebecca provides the structure, the support and the inspiration for her students to become artists. Through art, they make statements about current issues or issues they value and then reflect on the process with an artist statement; that tells why they choose their topic, what inspired them, what medium they choose and why and finally what they learned. The high expectations and the opportunities she provides for learning; help her students excel and produce high quality artwork.

Books on art for children:

Leonardo da Vinci for Kids, His Life and Ideas by Janis Herbert

Michelangelo: Getting to Know the World's Greatest Artists by Mike Venezla

Smart About Art: Pierre Auguste Renoir: Paintings That Smile by True Kelly

Frida Kahlo: The Artist Who Painted Herself by Margaret Firth

Jacob Lawrence: The Migration Series by Elizabeth Alexander

Claude Monet: Sunshine and Water Lilies by True Kelly

13 Artists Children Should Know by Angel Wenzel

Mary Cassatt: Family Pictures by Jane O'Connor

Women in Art: 50 Fearless Creatives Who Inspired the World by Rachel Ignotofsky

Pablo Picasso: Breaking All the Rules by True Kelley

Edgar Degas: Painting the Dance by Maryann Cocoa-Leffler

Jakes Makes a World: Jacob Lawrence, A Young Artist in Harlem by Sharifa Rhodes-Pitts

Children's Book of Art by DK

A Child's Introduction to Art: The World's Greatest Paintings and Sculptures by Heather Alexander

The Story of Painting: A History of Art for Children

The Arts: A Visual Encyclopedia by DK

Henri Matisse: Drawing with Scissors by Jane O'Connor

Vincent Van Gogh: Sunflowers and Swirly Stars by Joan Holui

Beautiful OOPS! By Barney Saltzberg and The Dot and Ish by Peter H. Reynolds

WAYS TO SUPPORT LEARNING

"Tell me and I forget, teach me and I remember, involve me and I learn." Benjamin Franklin (104)

If you have ever had someone explain how to do something on your computer by clicking here and then there and doing it for you, it will leave your head spinning, with no new information in it. In order to learn we need to see it, hear it, do it and then understand it. We must be ready for information, we need to be emotionally supported and calm, we must be well behaved and ready to listen.

Active Engagement

Most people are visual learners or learn best with a combination of visual and auditory learning, and if you can add a hands-on component you have an extremely effective learning strategy.

When we begin our study of the Earth, we read great books like The Restless Earth (105) by Melvin Berger and Earth: My First 4.54 Billion Years (Our Universe, Part 1) (106) by Stacy McAnulty. To provide a visual for students to better understand the Earth, we use a hard boiled egg. The shell is the Earth's crust, the egg white is the mantle and yolk is the core. To help students remember three parts of the Earth we make Earth candy. We use peppermint candy for the core (Candy=Core), we put the candy into the marshmallow or the mantle (Marshmallow=Mantle) and dip it into melted chocolate (Chocolate= Crust). To understand the movement of the Tectonic plates over the Earth's crust and mantle we use graham crackers and frosting to move the plates (graham crackers) to form Volcanoes, Mountains and Earthquakes across the mantle (frosting). Food does not always need to be involved to make learning interesting, but it does provide a delicious and helpful way to remember information.

Another example of hands-on learning is how we make Consonant-Vowel-Consonant (CVC) words on a mat that is divided into three columns. We have cards with letters, (vowels in red, consonants in black) which we give the children to use as we build words. We put the letters on the mat from left to right, and say the sound each letter makes as we build words. Then we sound the word out by blending the sounds together. Beginning with CVC words is an effective way for students to learn to decode words fairly quickly and provides an easy way to continue to make more words for students to read.

Gathering and Connecting Information

As teachers introduce a new subject, first, it is important to find out what your learners already know. This process helps the learner have a frame of reference and set the purpose for learning. When we begin our animal unit, we take a large roll of paper and write down everything we know about animals. We make headings with what animals need to live, like food, Oxygen, a habitat, and other animals. Below these headings we add all the information that we know for each heading. As we read this chart and look at all the things we already know about animals and then we make a list of questions we still have or things we want to learn and work on finding answers together. This process is very helpful since we are showing children how we talk through our thinking process; how we gather information and how we make connections between what we know and what we are learning.

Open Ended Questions

When encouraging students to be active participants in learning, phrasing questions is very important when helping children deepen their thinking. When you ask questions that are answered without much thought, there isn't much opportunity for thinking. When you ask open-ended questions like "What surprised you... How did you decide...? Or ask, "What questions do you have? ", it allows children to expand their thinking and adds a valuable discussion opportunity and helps them to become independent thinkers and helps them use open ended questions in small student led groups.

Children always amaze me with their ability to think deeply about topics, they have wonderful insights and are always curious about how and why things happen. I had a boy in Kindergarten class whose mother did not believe in God. He was constantly trying to figure out why she didn't believe, since he was learning about God and loved Him. As we discussed the actions of people throughout history, he wanted answers about how God could let things happen that were bad, why were some people mistreated or hurt. He wanted to know why some people were destined to be poor or slaves in a country or culture. He tried to understand his mother's reasons for not believing in God. To help him figure things out, we talked about how God has given us as His people the freedom to make choices and many times our collective and individual choices are not always good; but God is always there to help us. Throughout most of the school year whenever I would ask, "What questions do you have?", that was his. This type of independent thinking and constant search for answers is what learning is all about. We need to continue to ask questions with the urgency and frequency he did to help us figure out and learn more about our world and ourselves.

Scaffolds

Teachers provide scaffolds or supports for learners, to ensure they are confident to take a risk or ask a question and feel it is okay to make mistakes. When we begin having children write words, we model how we identify each sound as we break apart the word. We hold up a finger for each sound, make a line for each sound we hear on our white boards (which are easily erasable). We use our fingers again to identify and write each sound on the line and then sound out the word together. This process requires a lot of support and positive feedback for children to feel confident. Specific and helpful praise that tells children what they are doing well and what they have done that works. As learners become more confident, we can provide less support.

As students begin to write sentences and stories, we talk about how they will continue to use their fingers to identify each sound in a word. I have a set of alphabetical flip word cards that we use to find words that we need help spelling and then add to our writing word bank.

The most effective method for helping students write independently is to tell them, "To write what you hear." This "push them out of the nest" method or removing the scaffold helps them write what they hear and not worry if words are spelled correctly. Children who are reluctant to write independently and ask for teacher support usually progress more slowly when writing, than those students who jump out of the nest and begin to write independently. As children write and read more, their word familiarity increases and their writing improves. Like anything else, the more you practice, the better you get. After we read stories together, we complete story maps or write about the book in our journals. We read wonderful books by many authors; we talk about the events, the characters, the problem and how it was solved. We make predictions about what might happen next. We make connections to books we have read and connections to our lives. We talk about how writers write about things they love and know about. We fill a paper heart with all the things that are important to us that may eventually be used in stories. We read books about how writers create stories.

Books about the writing process:
Plot Chickens by Mary Jane Anch,

From Picture to Words: A Book About Making a Book by Janet Stevens,

Little Red Writing by Joan Holub,

Author: A True Story by Helen Lester,

The Best Story by Eileen Spinelli and

Ralph Tells a Story by Abby Hanlon

EXPLORATION

STEAM (107) (Science, Technology, Engineering, Arts and Mathematics) activities are perfect for children to invent, create or figure out how an existing invention works and how an invention can be useful in a real life setting.

STEAM has become such an important component of learning that companies develop these products for classrooms and home learning. In our town we have a learning store that is dedicated to exposing children to the thinking and problem solving process that STEAM encourages.

At school, we have a variety of STEAM activities including very popular magnetic pattern blocks. Pattern blocks are blocks we use for teaching shapes, patterns, and symmetry, as they are always standard size and color and shapes such as: hexagons, triangles, rhombus, trapezoids and squares.

These magnetic pattern blocks allow for a never-ending ability to create three- dimensional objects that become homes for animals, or a spaceship, a community or anything else at that moment of creative construction. These STEAM activities encourage and excite children to become inventors and critical thinkers.

Each year during open house I have parents participate in some type of STEAM activity. It not only provides a great activity for parents to get to know one another and work together, but also allows them to understand the value of the activities for children and appreciate the collaborative process and communication needed to complete these activities.

Books to Inspire:

Iggy Peck, Architect, Rosie Revere, Engineer and Iggy Peck's Big Project Book for Amazing Architects all by Andrea Beaty

The Most Magnificent Thing by Ashley Spires

The Three Little Pigs, An Architectural Tale by Steven Guarnaccia

The Noisy Paintbox: The Colors and Sounds of Kandinsky's Abstract Art by Barb Rosenstock,

Awesome Engineering Activities for Kids: 50+ Exciting STEAM to Design and Build by Christina Schul and

On a Beam of Light, A Story of Albert Einstein by Jennifer Berne

Mistakes That Worked: 40 Familiar Inventions & How They Came to Be by Charlotte Foltz Jones

The Way Things Work by David MaCauley

11 Experiments that Failed by Jenny Offill

Mechanimals by Chris Tougas

Who Says Women Can't be Doctors?: The Story of Elizabeth Blackwell by Tanya Lee Stone

The Girl Who Thought in Pictures: The Story of Dr. Temple Grandin by Julia Finley Mosca

Grace Hopper: Queen of Computer Code by Laurie Wallmark

Margaret and the Moon by Dean Robbins

Solving the Puzzle Under the Sea: Marie Tharp Maps the Ocean Floor by Robert Burleigh

<u>Shark Lady: The True Story of How Eugenie Clark Became the Ocean's Most Fearless Scientist</u> by Jess Keeting

<u>Look Up: Henrietta Leavitt, Pioneering Woman Astronomer</u> by Robert Burleigh

<u>Caroline's Comets: A True Story</u> by Emily Arnold McCully

REMOTE LEARNING

Thankfully, our daughters are technologically skilled and are always up to date on new and innovative technology for learning and help us effectively add technology to our classroom instruction. This fall, we added Seesaw, a learning platform, as a way to share pictures of projects we were completing in school with parents, as well as a way for students to complete some lessons independently. When we began our stay at home orders, my husband and I brought home all our weekly book bins for both our class for fours and the Kindergarten class. With the help of a homemade video stand, and our girls as additional readers, we began recording lessons, reading books, and teaching new math games and science and social science lessons to upload to Seesaw. The Seesaw learning platform allows students to send back a recording of their reading, or a recording to tell what they learned, as well as a way to return a math page or journal entry for feedback. (web.Seesaw.me)

With these online lessons our Kindergarten class continued learning very effectively and the addition of our "learning box" of materials for each unit allowed my students to have as close to an in school experience as possible. We continued our unit on Women's History, and began new instruction on simple machines, The Earth, Rocks, Dinosaurs, Delaware and Lewes History, we completed our Values unit while continuing math instruction to include a review of fractions, money and time with books and video support. Our Kindergarten children continued their spelling lessons, reading with leveled book bags and continued practicing passages from their fluency books, they worked on their Fry list of words, listed facts they learned in response to a nonfiction book or used their journal for creative writing and even completed cold reads or new passages for evaluation. I am extremely grateful for the support our daughters and our children's parents provided for this online learning experience. The key to successful remote learning is creative teaching and curriculum specific lessons, learning materials, parental support, flexibility, and a positive attitude.

With uncertainty about returning to school in the fall, many schools are investigating ways to make remote learning more effective for students and more manageable for families. Parents need to remember that this change in our learning is hopefully temporary and that most do have the tools to support invest in and supplement their child or children's learning at home. It may look different, it may be more difficult, but learning is more than traditional school curriculum and as my Kindergarten families in particular exemplified, remote learning can provide memorable learning experiences.

Home learning still depends on parent support, especially with preschool aged and elementary school children. With so many variables, it is hard to predict a clear path for in school education to safely resume. I understand that it may be impossible for some parents due to work schedules and stressful for others to assume the additional role of teacher to their role as parent and provider. Remote learning is impossible for those without computers or Internet connections.

Remember, learning is not just worksheets and memorizing information, it should be about understanding broad concepts and ideas, understanding historical events of our country, the impact they have had on our world, and how the events of the world shape our lives. Learning should be about: understanding how things work and learning should include meaningful activities; like watching the incubation process of baby chicks and then watch as they grow and produce eggs themselves, using real measurements to build a tree house in the backyard, or real and useful measurements to bake a cake, or make lasagna. Families could take learning outside and dig a hole to install a pond. You could raise pond plants and fish. You could scoop up some tadpoles and watch them as they turn into frogs and add them to your pond. Your family could adopt a highway or road and work to keep it clean.

We can look to Alexis Loveraz, a 16- year old student for inspiration for creating a platform for successful remote learning. He had been tutoring student through snap chat and text messaging and decided to create TikTok instructional videos for algebra, geometry and chemistry during the stay at home orders to reduce the spread of the Covid-19. He has effectively reached and helped 650,000 students and has even added an SAT preparation class for students preparing for an upcoming test. His creative approach to helping others is commendable. (108)

I am also not naive in assuming that remote learning will work for all learners and all populations. The need for remote learning due to school closings to lessen the spread of Covid-19, further exposed the inequality of educational systems in poorer communities to people who live outside those communities. These communities need our attention and resources.

In general, school districts struggled to provide devices and Internet services to teach children and adequately support their learning. To lessen the achievement gap caused by school closures, our local school district slowed the delivery of assignments to students, while they worked to get computers and Internet services to families who needed them. Curriculum was also trimmed to reduce the amount of time students were on computers.

The transition from in school learning and remote learning was an adjustment and at times difficult for students and teachers alike.

New rules and procedures were not only discovered to be necessary, but also needed to be taught to students to make remote learning effective.

Many parents didn't have the choice to stay home to support remote learning, but had to go to work to provide food and shelter for their families. While some parents enjoyed the privilege of working from home and were available to not just support their child's learning but enrich their learning with experiments, books and activities.

Both our girls work in schools where a majority of the population is economically disadvantaged and the ability of these students to learn remotely was negatively affected by lack of Internet and available family support.

As we share our concern for safely opening schools, remember that learning is broader than classroom walls and that many can supplement learning at home for their children with books, games, experiments, research projects and creative solutions. I believe our focus and resources should be on helping children in communities where parents cannot afford to stay home, or cannot afford to create a safe home learning pod for their children with a group of families and a private teacher. Many children depend on the school for a healthy breakfast and lunch; others depend on special services for learning disabilities, for speech and language therapy, for occupational therapy and for counseling. Maybe these children need to safely return to school. Every model that is presented will not be equitable to everyone, but Covid-19, has disproportionately affected communities of color and low-income communities, and that is certainly not fair. I think 2020 is a year of exceptions, a year to look beyond ourselves and try to take care of those whose daily lives are filled with struggles and inequalities and find creative solutions to bridge the gaps of inequality.

What role do we have in demanding effective and comprehensive education for all children in a safe environment?

78 Learning and the Adolescent Mind. Community of LearnersLearningandtheadolescentmind.com

79 Smith, Katie Milway, 2008 One Hen. Goodreads.com

80Onehen.org

81 Choi, Yangsook, 2003 penguinrandomhousebooks.com

82 Kids, Lonely Planet, 2015. Amazon.com

83 Songland., 2020 nbc.com

84 Village, The 2019 nbc.com

85 teacherspayteachers.com

86 McGill, Bryant H. Brainyquote.com

87 Eger, Edith Dr., 2018 Dreditheger.com

88 Einstein, Albert, 2016 Quoteinvestigatoe.com

89 Emily, 2017. Educationtothecore.com

90 Coelho, Paulo, 2019 paulocoelho.com

91 Dweck, Carol Dr., 2007 Mondsetworks.com

92 Obama, Barack, 2020 Virtual Graduation nytimes.com

93 Emerson, Ralph Waldo inspiringquotes.com

94 Waldorf, Sarah and Stephan, Annelisa, 2020 Blogs.getty.edu

95 Voyager, Boston, 2018 bostonvoyager.com

96 Pepper, Jen. 2011 The Chatty Press Design Co.

97 Fair, Molly, 2010 Communityjusticeexchange.org

98 Talk Killing of George Floyd, 2020 en.wikipedia.org

99 Parents Scholastic, 2018 bookfairs.scholastic.com

100 The New York Times Upfront

101 Science in School The European Journal for Science Teachers. Scienceinschools.com

102 Howell, Elizabeth, 2020 NASA's Hidden Figures Space.com

103 Scholastic ART Classroommagazines.com

104 Franklin, Benjamin. Brainyquote.com

105 Berger, Melvin, 1996 The Restless Earth amazon.com

106 McAnulty, Stacy. Stacymcnaulty.com

107 STEAM steampoweredfamily.com

108 New York 2020, Turoringnewyork.cbslocal.com

PART 4:

PAUSE AND RESOLVE

Pause by definition is a temporary rest.

Resolve by definition means to firmly decide on a course of action.

In March of 2020, our normal lives were paused. For some, we used this time as an opportunity to reflect on: our lives and our actions, our faith, and our resolve. Some used this time to reflect on the effects and utter despair we felt as the novel and lethal Coronavirus floated around the globe killing vulnerable people. Some of us used this time to assess our values and beliefs, to determine our role in racism and to comprehend the senseless, tragic deaths of people due to the color of their skin that we witnessed via television. Others used this time to watch the protesters urging for the critical need for systemic changes to our laws and their enforcement and fair treatment for all people- from the safety of their homes, while some marched. We paused to reflect how we can strengthen our resolve to make positive changes in our lives and our communities and how we can become more accepting and compassionate people. Others paused to teach children and support their learning with creative, innovative lessons, books and games.

Our pause also allowed us the opportunity to look at our environment, climate change and how ecosystems all around the world seemed better off with us sheltered in place. We had time to think about the negative impact and damage we have caused to our environment, the constant threat of climate change, and our need to investigate and then determine how and if our imprint on our world helped spread the virus. Does our continuous claiming of land, as we encroach on animals' habitats, make us more susceptible to diseases that animals harbor? Does the destruction of wildlife habitats allow disease to find its way to us? Does global warming impact the spread of this virus? Our pause should have allowed us to look more directly at the health of our planet and how our planet's health affects our health.

While sheltering in place, we had time to reflect on how our country and state leaders have handled Covid-19 as it raced through vulnerable populations with a high number of fatalities, and as it ravaged economic and educational opportunities of people from those same communities. We had time to improve our ability to test, trace, isolate and treat people with Covid-19, but we needed financial resources and support from the Federal Government. Ironically, we have the resources to test players from major league teams on a daily basis, but not our vulnerable populations returning to work.

For others, who just recently have been labeled as "essential workers"- our doctors and nurses, those who work as bus drivers, sanitation workers, maintenance and cleaning workers, postal workers and grocery store workers- rushed into action to protect us, transport us, deliver goods to our houses and to feed us. They did not get a pause.

The epidemiologists and medical professionals worked tirelessly to learn about this invisible and deadly virus, to help treat those infected and to create guidelines to educate us on how we can "flatten the curve" and protect our communities- did not get a pause. We thanked them with gift cards, and clapping, we thanked them with signs and banners. But as the weather got warm, we lost our "collective" resolve to fight and contain this virus and keep our vulnerable populations safe. Families wanted to get out, have their children socialize with friends, eat dinner at their favorite restaurant, meet with their book club, or have their child attend a sports camp, some without hot and uncomfortable masks.

While some people from our most vulnerable populations continued to work in dangerous jobs, often without adequate or any personal protective equipment, and with the constant worry about bringing Covid-19 home to loved ones. Our exhausted and emotionally taxed health care workers continued to fight daily, while we lost our resolve to slow the spread of the virus.

Since we lost our "collective" resolve to wear masks, physically distance, wash our hands and stay home, we haven't controlled the virus: we aren't able to give essential workers a pause, or provide safe working environments for many workers, including teachers. We also haven't been able to establish a national plan to open schools safely that includes funding, testing and tracing or to find creative solutions to implement effective remote or hybrid learning for all children. We tired too easily- we lost our resolve.

Our pause should have allowed us time to look at our nursing homes and the essential workers who work within nursing homes. These workers are often underpaid and need to work two jobs to piece together a meager income. Did we provide them with financial assistance and adequate PPE? Could they bring in the virus from another job into the nursing home? Are air filters and air conditioners circulating infected air from room to room?

Our pause should have allowed us to look at our justice system and overcrowded prisons and determine that non-violent drug offenders should be in a program that provides them with the help they need. The pause should have allowed us time to investigate the disproportionate number of people of color sentenced to jail terms inconsistent to the severity of their crimes and resolve these problems.

Our pause should have allowed us time to look at our healthcare system and our ability to keep people healthy and not be reactive when they become sick. Not surprisingly many people with underlying diseases are dying more readily than those who are healthier. Our pause should have allowed us time to look at our vulnerable populations and find solutions to improve their health. We know that a healthy diet, good medical care, vaccinations, yearly dental health check ups, exercise, sleep and a safe working environment all lead to a more healthy population. We tired too easily.

Our pause <u>did</u> allow us time to protest for systemic changes in our government and law enforcement, to work to ensure our laws and police protect all people equally and fairly. Our pause allowed us to raise our voice for change. The Black Lives Matter protesters did not pause, they continue with valiant determination that exemplifies the example John Lewis' life and his courage provided us.

Our pause allowed major league teams to delay their seasons to protest social injustice and negotiate the use of stadiums for safe voting facilities.

Today, John Lewis' body traveled across the infamous Edmund Pettus Bridge for the last time. As we reflect on his life, we are reminded how his constant and continuous resolve helped us create a world that was a little more fair and a little more just for all people. John Lewis exemplified courage and resolve and told us to continue to work together until we create a "Beloved Community" of equality. He saw the good in people and never wavered from his idea that people could change their hearts. (109)

In 2009, events proved Lewis' belief correct that people could change their hearts as Elwin Wilson; a reformed Ku Klux Klansman met with John Lewis to apologize for beating him on May 9, 1961. Lewis and Albert Bigelow waited in a "for whites only" waiting room during a stop on the "Freedom Riders" bus trail, whose riders fought to change segregation laws on interstate buses. Four white men, one of whom was Wilson, savagely beat Lewis and Bigelow. John Lewis not only accepted Wilson's apology, but also toured with him to share the power of forgiveness and a person's ability to change their heart. (110)

Lewis' final crossing of the Pettus bridge symbolized his lifelong ability to reach out and bridge the divide between people of all races, of all genders and all sexual orientation. His celebration of life echoed his resolve to always work towards a more equitable world with tireless determination. A quote from his 2017 memoir, "Across the Bridge: A Vision for Change and the Future of America", (111) encourages us to continue our fight for equality and that we will never truly be free until we are all treated equally with these words, "Freedom is not a state; it is an act. It is not an enchanted garden perched high on a distant plateau where we can finally sit down to rest. Freedom is the continuous action we all must take, and each generation must do its part to create an even more fair, and more just society." Thank you, John Lewis for not tiring too easily.

As we begin the process of rectifying the complicated events and problems that have led to injustice, inequality, oppression, and illness throughout our existence, we need the resolve to do better and work together. Our country needs to invest in all communities and areas vulnerable to poverty, unemployment, injustices and inequality: by improving our educational systems and by providing learning opportunities for young children, by increasing funding to ensure high quality teaching and learning across the country for all students, by increasing funding for school counselors, nurses, school psychologists and social workers, by teaching all children more than reading and math, with sparse lessons on history and science.

By helping all children take advantage of every opportunity and experience they have to learn, we can make a difference.

We can make a difference in our towns and cities as they recruit and hire police officers from within their communities, so they are part of the community and are invested in working with and protecting the members of that community. By upholding the 14th Amendment that guarantees equal protection under the law for all Americans, we can make a difference.

We can make a difference by providing Social Services to all communities, to help stop the violence and abuse that may be experienced at home, and to use skills and training to empower people to qualify for, obtain and keep jobs.

We can make a difference by de-stigmatizing mental health problems and then provide necessary support. We can make a difference when we create a healthcare system that proactively keeps people healthy, instead of reactively treating them when they are sick.

When we allocate effort, resources and regulations to protect the health of our planet, preserve wildlife habitats and recycle and reuse resources more effectively, we can make a positive step toward a healthy Earth.

We can make a difference when our church communities think and act like Jesus, with love and acceptance for all, the unloved, the forgotten, the oppressed and the impoverished.

We can make a difference by creating communities with inclusion for all, in our schools, businesses, churches, government offices and in our homes. We can make a difference when we abolish laws that unfairly oppress and disproportionately imprison people of color.

We can make a difference when we invest in the potential of all people.

Rhode Island Governor Gina M. Raimondo and Back To Work RI (112) will use 45 million dollars in financial funding from the CARES Act to partner with local businesses who will train and employ the economically vulnerable who lost jobs due to Covid-19. Raimondo and Mike Grey,

Chair of the Governor's Workforce Board will work with John Hope Bryant, founder of Operation HOPE (113), and Zoe Baird, CEO and President of the Markle Foundation (114) along with private businesses who will match talent with jobs. Every participating employer will sign a pledge to train each participant to ensure they have the tools they need to succeed and get hired. This program offers wrap around services that provide language support, counseling, financial coaching, childcare, transportation and access to technology. Franklin D. Roosevelt's Civilian Conservation Corp (CCC) (115) provided hope during the Great Depression to people facing eviction, poverty and hunger due to unemployment. Back to Work RI provides an amazing opportunity for the state and businesses to invest in the potential of the people of Rhode Island and also provides a working model for all states to emulate as they plan to invest in the potential of all people in their communities. Delaware announced a similar program to effectively support those unemployed due to the effects of Covid-19.

As we improve the systems that were created to educate, protect, heal and support the people of our country, we need to provide extensive training to those who implement these services and hold people accountable for the effectiveness and fairness of these services and institutions. As we tackle and mend our weaknesses and repair the fault lines of inequality throughout our country with strength, empathy, justice, character, determination and grit, we will build a stronger, better future for all.

We can learn from Helen Keller's eloquent words, "Character cannot be developed in ease and quiet. Only through experience of trial and suffering can the soul be strengthened, ambition inspired, and success achieved." (116)

Many have suffered, but we can be inspired and strengthened by all the peaceful protesters, whose ambition and resolve will help lead us to positive change. People who have always treated others with respect and love can strengthen us. We remember all who have died at the hands of injustice, all who have died in the fight for justice. We honor all who have worked tirelessly and endlessly for change with the determination to stand firm in the fundamental values and beliefs of our country to demand and promote positive change and elevate our ability to be a more perfect union.

As we teach our children kindness, empathy, and to act in ways that make us better and more hopeful, as a people and as a nation, we can do this in small bites, connect our loops and cooperate, be accountable for your talk and your actions, raise your voice and be heard, and actively work to resolve problems.

Abraham Lincoln said, "Be sure to put your feet in the right place, and stand firm."(117) We need to heed his advice. We need to know and understand the promise of our Constitution to be a united nation. We need live the pledge we make to the flag as a symbol of all who bravely fought and continue to fight for our freedom and equality:

I pledge (promise) allegiance (loyalty and devotion) to the flag

Of the United States of America,

And to the Republic (government where we elect our leaders) for which it stands,One Nation, under God, indivisible (not able to be divided, but to stick together) with liberty (freedom) and justice (fair treatment) for all.

We need to put our feet in the right place, but keep moving for positive change, we need to not be divided, but to stick together and fight for freedom and fair treatment for all.

President Barack Obama's speech at the Democratic National Convention was moving and direct. He both framed the enduring purpose of the Constitution as well and the imperfections of the Constitution by saying, "I am in Philadelphia, where the Constitution was drafted and signed. It wasn't a perfect document. It allowed for the inhumanity

176

of slavery and failed to guarantee women and even men who didn't own property the right to participate in the political process. But embedded in this document was a North Star that would guide future generations. A system of representative government, a democracy with which we could better realize our highest ideals. Through, Civil War and bitter struggles we improved this Constitution to include the voices of those who had once been left out.

Gradually we made this country more just, more equal and more free."(118) He spoke how the president's job is to protect, preserve and defend not just our freedom, but also the ideals Americans have fought for and died for. He spoke to the urgent responsibility that we have to vote- to not just preserve our democracy, but to make us better as people and a nation. His speech was a call to action that threaded the theme of the convention intent that- We the People can work together to build back a better future for all people.

William H. Hastie's words remind us, "Democracy is a process, not a static condition. It is becoming rather than being. It can be easily lost, but is never fully won. Its essence is eternal struggle." (119)

In Michelle Obama's speech at the 2020 Democratic National Convention, she referenced the failure of our current leadership to protect Americans from Covid-19 and the economic, emotional and educational anguish caused by its wrath. (120) She referenced social and racial injustices ignored by current leaders that continue to occur in our country as black Americans are murdered in plain sight, who then label those who protest these murders as enemies of the state and try to silence their cries with tear gas and rubber bullets. She gently referenced the lack of leadership that caused the erosion of our economy, and of our healthcare system and the blatant disregard of the basic premise that each American life has worth. She said, "Because whenever we look at the White House for some leadership or consolation or any semblance of steadiness, what we get instead is chaos, division, and a total and utter lack of empathy." She said,... "We can still believe in the goodness and grace in our households and neighborhoods all across our nation"... and... " We have the power to change things and work together to find a way to live together and work together across our differences." She cautioned us to make sure our children know that when, " they see entitlement that says only certain people belong here, that greed is good, and winning is everything as long as you come out on top, it doesn't matter what happened to everyone else.".... We send a dangerous message and tear apart the integrity and the soul of our nation. But she also has hope and optimism in our ability to change our future when she said, "It is up to us to add our voices and our votes to the course of history."

...."And if we want to keep the possibility of progress alive in our time, if we want to be able to look our children in the eye after this election, we have got to reassert our place in American history." We need to vote for a decent man. She told us, " We have got to grab our comfortable shoes, put on our masks, pack a brown bag dinner and maybe breakfast too, because we've got to be willing to stand in line all night if we have to."

Let us stay vigilant in the struggle to create an inclusive country that welcomes and cares for everyone. Vote responsibly for candidates willing to make the changes you seek, beginning with our Mayors, District Attorneys and our Representatives, our Governors and legislators and finally our President. Our vote is our voice. Voting is one way to fight for the kind of world we want for our children.

As Joe Biden eloquently accepted the Democratic nomination for America's President of the United States he emphasized that he will be the bond of unity that will bring us out of the darkness. His words give us hope that together we can heal the vast divide that tears the fabric of our country apart: by protecting Americans from Covid-19 as we responsibly follow science and work together to lessen the spread by following the simple guidelines set forth to protect us, by unraveling, addressing and healing systemic racism, by bolstering American jobs for the middle class, by working diligently to lessen the effects of climate change on our environment and by working together to be a better, more united, more understanding and compassionate United States of America. His words echo the hope our founding fathers had as they worked collaboratively to form a representative, though imperfect, democracy that evolves and changes and continuously moves toward a more perfect and inclusive union. He said, " Make no mistake. United we can, and will overcome this season of darkness in America. We will choose hope over fear, facts over fiction, fairness over privilege." He addressed our ability to face and resolve inequality that has long gripped our nation when he said; "History has thrust one more urgent task on us." "Will we be the generation that finally wipes the stain of racism from our national character?" "This is our movement." "This is our mission. May history be able to say that the end of the chapter of American darkness began here tonight, as love and hope and light joined in the battle for the soul of our nation. And this is the battle that we together will win."(121)

Biden's speech encapsulated and strengthened the theme of the convention *We the People*, the time honored words of promise stated in our Constitution of the United States of America, that provide us with the promise that we together can continue to work to form a more perfect union and work together to secure the blessings of liberty for all Americans for all posterity.

RIPPLES OF HOPE

The book <u>Each Kindness </u>(122) by Jacqueline Woodson, tells a story of Maya, a girl in ragged clothing who begins school midyear. Maya tries to befriend students in her new class, by sharing her jacks, or playing cards at recess. Each time she tries to share, she is faced with turned heads, whispers and taunts. One day in the spring, Maya comes to school in a nice hand me down dress and sandals, her classmates continue to be hurtful and give her a new nickname of "Nothing New". The next day, Maya is not at school. That same day, Ms. Albert, the teacher, has a big bowl of water and a stone for each child. As she puts the first stone in the water, she explains to the children that as waves ripple from the stone, this is what kindness does. Each little kind thing we do goes out like a ripple out into the world. Ms. Albert asks each child to tell something they have done to show kindness as they drop their stone into the bowl. The girl who narrates the story holds onto her stone, since she can't think of anything kind she has done. Holding her stone, she begins to regret that she treated Maya unkindly. One afternoon on her way home, she stops at the pond and throws stone after stone into the pond. Each stone signifies the kindness she should have shown Maya. She regrets missing her chance to be kind.

This is such a clear lesson about how our actions and words cause ripples that spread out into the world. We have the choice to decide what type of ripples we send.

As we think about the ripples we create. We need to continue to ask ourselves questions. Do we really believe that one person's life is more valuable than another's life? Do we really believe that divisiveness and hostility will solve the problems we face? Do we really believe we can continue to ignore or be indifferent to the needs of others as we continue to live well? Do we believe that our supportive words are enough to make changes in systemic racism without changing our laws and policies?

We are the leaders our children see and emulate. What type of leaders do we want our children to become?

John Lewis' words remind us that every one of us can make a difference. In an article "Together, you can redeem the soul of our nation", published on the day of his funeral, John Lewis said, "I may not be here with you, I urge you to answer the highest calling of your heart and stand up for what you believe. In my life I have done all I can to demonstrate that the way of peace, the way of love and nonviolence is the more excellent way. Now it is your turn to let freedom ring."(123)

After Jean Williamson's son Jacob Blake was shot seven times in the back by police, she made an impassioned plea for peace and for all people to examine their hearts. She voiced how her son would not appreciate the violence and unrest in response to his shooting.

Her gentle but powerful words send everyone a message of hope and inclusion that can not be denied.

She said, "As I pray for my son's healing; physically, emotionally and spiritually- I also have been praying even before this for the healing of our country. God has placed each and every one of us here in this country because He wanted us here. Clearly you can see by now that I have beautiful brown skin. But take a look at your hand. Whatever shade it is, it is beautiful as well. How dare we hate what we are. We are humans. God did not make one type of tree or flower or fish or horse or grass or rock. How dare you ask Him to make one type of human that looks just like you." (124)

She was speaking to all of us as her words emphasized that no one race or people are superior. God is the only supreme being.

Her words echo the words of heroic leaders when she told us, "Let's use our hearts, our love, and our intelligence to work together, to show the rest of the world how humans are supposed to treat each other. America is great when we behave greatly."

It is our turn to take positive steps to be more accepting, more compassionate, and to be a positive example for our children in both our actions and our words. We need to raise our children to be optimistic, resilient and to know that they can make a difference with kind words and actions.

We need to be responsible neighbors and citizens by wearing our masks and by doing all we can to protect vulnerable populations. We need to stand firm in our convictions and be firm in our faith. We need to answer the highest calling of our hearts and decide what we can do to fight for the world we want for our children and resolve to do our part to raise hopeful children in our changing world.

Nelson Mandela said, "You can start changing our world for the better daily, no matter how small the action." (125) Today is the day!

109 Tensely, Brandon and Stacqualursi, Veronica, 2020 cnn.com

110 Dys, Andrew, 2015 Heraldonline.com

111 Lewis, John, 2017 Across That Bridge barnsandnoble.com

112 Office of the Governor, 2020 RI.gov

113 Operation HOPE operationhope.org

114 Markle, We stand with Others to Condemn Racism, Discrimination and Injustice

Markle.com

115 Civilian Conservation Corps. En.wikipedia.org

116 Keller, Helen brainyquote.com

117 Lehrman, Lewis E., 2017 wjs.com

118 Obama, Barack, 2020 cnn.com

119 Hastie, William H. What is Democracy? Facinghistory.org

https://www.facinghistory.org/resource-library/what-democracy

120 Wilkie, Christina, 2020 cnbc.com

121 Watch Market, 2020 Joe Biden's DNC speech Marketwatch.com

122 Woodson, Jacqueline, 2012 Each Kindness. Barnsandnoble.com

123 Lewis, John 2020 orlandosentinel.com

124 Williamson, Jean 2020,insider.com

125 India.com staff, 2020 India.com

WORKS CITED:

1. Confucius. Quotes.net. https://www.quotes.net/quote50140

2.Twain, Mark. (N.D.). Quotable Quote. Goodreads.com https://www.goodreads.com/quotes/539027-never-argue-with-stupid-people-they-will-drag-you-down

3. Young, Ed. (2002, June 10). PuffinRandomhouse.com https://www.penguinrandomhouse.com/books/290804/seven-blind-mice-by-ed-young-illustrated-by-ed-young/

4.AJMC. (2006 Nov.). Impact of co-pays on vulnerable populations. The American Journal of Managed Care, Vol. 12 (No. 13), S359-S363. https://cdn.sanity.io/files/0vv8moc6/ajmc/a6e63020988960c0ae4f73aa2e7a4af3c3c8c76d.pdf

5 Kia's Accelerate the Good Program. (2020, April 9). Supporting Homeless Youth During This Crisis. Youtube.com https://www.youtube.com/watch?v=keyruF6XLdw

6. 10 Thought Provoking Lessons from Mahatma Gandhi. (2012, April) www.writechangegrow.com

7.Stoetz, William (2019, September 28)/ Quora. https://wwwquora.com

8 Biography.com Editors. (2020, June 1). Inspiring Martin Luther King Jr. Quotes. Biography.com.https://www.biography.com/news/martin-luther-king-famous-quotes

9 Juma, Norbert (2020, June 26). 60 Fredrick Douglass Quotes about Freedom and Progress, everydaypower.com https://everydaypower.com/frederick-douglass-quotes/

10 History.com Editors,

U.S. Slavery: Timeline, Figures & Abolition- HISTORY. (2020, July 6). Slavery in America. History.com. https://www.history.com/topics/black-history/slavery

11 Mitchell, Tia. (2020, June 1).

Reactions mixed after Rep. John Lewis rebukes protect violence. Ajc.com https://www.ajc.com/news/state--regional-govt--politics/reac-tions-mixed-after-rep-john-lewis-rebukes-protest-violence/ QsMOR05l0T1R3BJ2fmIkeI/

12 Atwell, Ashleigh Lakieva. (2018, January 2018).

Songwriter Who Wrote "We Shall Overcome" Finally Gets Credit For Her Work Blavity.com https://blavity.com/songwriter-who-wrote-we-shall-overcome-final-ly-gets-credit-for-her-work?category1=news&category2=black-history

13 Adams, Noah. (2013, August 28).

The Inspiring Force of 'We Shall Overcome". Nrp.org. https://www.npr.org/2013/08/28/216482943/the-inspiring-force-of-we-shall-overcome

14 Talk. (2020, August 20 edited) (UTC)

Wikipedia. En.winkipedia.org https://en.wikipedia.org/wiki/ Lean on Me (song)

15 History.Com Editors. (2009, October 27 updated 2020, April 8).

Brown vs. board of education. History.com https://www.history.com/topics/black-history/brown-v-board-of-education-of-topeka

16 Obsessed (2014, May 28).

16 Unforgettable Things Maya Angelo Wrote and Said. Glamour.com https://www.glamour.com/story/maya-angelou-quotes

Works cited

17 Scully, Kristina. (2020).

Pathway2Success. Thepathway2success.com. https://www.thepathway2success.com

18 Kiger, Patrick J. (2020, February 11) 8 Things We Know About Crispus Attucks.

History.com https://www.history.com/news/ crispus-attucks-american-revolution-boston-massacre

19 Stowe, Harriet Beecher. (1852) ISBN 978-1508480129

Amazon.com https://www.amazon.com/Uncle-Cabin-Harriet-Beecher-Stowe/ dp/1508480125

20 Lincoln, Abraham: The Emancipation Proclamation. (1863, January 1). Archives.gov. https://www.archives.gov/exhibits/featured-documents/emancipation-proclamation

21 Jefferson, Thomas. (1776, July 4).
Declaration of Independence: A Transcription
Archives.gov https://www.archives.gov/founding-docs/declaration-transcript

22 Bleiberg, Larry. (2018, July 22).
Witness a history of racial injustice at two new museums in Alabama and Mississippi. Latimes.com https://www.latimes.com/travel/la-tr-alabama-mississippi-museums-20180722-story.html

23 McGarrity, Steven. (2020, June 19).
Juneteenth: A time for celebrations, but also re-commitment.
Community Legal Aid.org. https://www.communitylegalaid.org/node/1297/juneteenth-time-celebration-also-re-commitment

24 Black Lives Matter website. Blacklivesmatter.com.
https://blacklivesmatter.com

25 Foston, Cheryl. (2013, January 2).
Light Up the Darkness. Whatcherylersaid: wordpress.com.
https://whatcherylsaid.wordpress.com/2013/01/02/light-up-the-darkness/

26 Rodenhizer, Samuel. (2018, January 15)
Quotation Celebration. Quotationcelebration.wordpress.com
https://quotationcelebration.wordpress.com/2018/01/15/the-measure-of-intelligence-is-the-ability-to-change-albert-einstein/

27 Little, Becky. (2018, December 4)
"Unbought and Unbossed": Why Shirley Chisholm Ran for President.
History.com. https://www.history.com/news/shirley-chisholm-presidential-campaign-george-wallace

28 Blackpast. (2013, January 22)
George Wallace, "Segregation Now, Segregation Forever"
Blackpast.com https://www.blackpast.org/african-american-history/speeches-african-american-history/1963-george-wallace-segregation-now-segregation-forever/

29 Cline-Ransome, Lesa. (2020, January 14).(The Power of Her Pen 1)
Publisher: Simon and Schuster/Paula Wiseman Books

https://www.simonandschuster.com/books/The-Power-of-Her-Pen/
Lesa-Cline-Ransome/9781481462891

30 Ocasio-Cortez, Alexandria. (2020, July 3). Alexandria Ocasio-Cortez
Responds to Ted Yoho's Apology on the House Floor. Youtube.com
https://www.youtube.com/watch?v=xJBczqHiSx8

31 Khalid, Asma. (2020, August 12). Joe Biden and Kamala Harris make Joint
Appearance. Npr.org Joe Biden And Kamala Harris Make 1st Joint Appearance

32 Woodward, Aylin. (2020, January 3).
Greta Thunberg turns 17 today. Here's how she started a global climate movement in Just 18 months.
Businessinsider.com https://www.businessinsider.com/
greta-thunberg-bio-climate-change-activist-2019-9

33 Solly, Meilan. (2020, June 4). 158 Resources To Understand Racism
in America.smithsonianmag.com https://www.smithsonianmag.com/
history/158-resources-understanding-systemic-racism-america-180975029/

34 Hakim, Joy. (2011, May 4). A History of US- Volumes.KAA, Inc. abebooks.
com https://www.abebooks.com/servlet/BookDetailsPL?bi=30710234273&cm_
mmc=ggl-_-COM_DSAETAFEED_Rare-_-naa-_-naa&gclid=Cj0KCQjws536BR
DTARIsANeUZ59HtzvC92doDPqERAlEmHj4_2bFub1TttTBEx5zZxyxe6hBuQ0
DU7oaAubzEALw_wcB

35 Bryan, Ashley (2016, September 13). Freedom over me: Eleven slaves, their
lives and dreams brought to life. Edition 1) simonansschuster.com
https://www.simonandschuster.com/books/Freedom-Over-Me/
Ashley-Bryan/9781481456906

36 Fitzgerald, F. Scott. Treasurequotes.com https://www.treasurequotes.com/
quotes/strength-shows-not-only-in-the-ability-to-pers

37 Carter, Jimmy and Rosalynn. (2020, June 3) Former President. Jimmy Carter's
statement on George Floyd's Death. www.cnn.com
https://www.cnn.com/2020/06/03/politics/jimmy-carter-george-floyd-statement/
index.html

38 King, Martin Luther, Jr. (1964) Nobel Prize acceptance speech Stockholm,
Sweden. Mlk.wsu.edu https://mlk.wsu.edu/about-dr-king/famous-quotes/

39 Floyd, Terrance transcript. (2020, June 1). Terrance Floyd,
Brother of George Floyd, Memorial Prayer Transcript At Site of

Floyd's Death. Rev.com https://www.rev.com/blog/transcripts/
terrence-floyd-brother-of-george-floyd-prayer-transcript-at-site-of-floyds-death
40 Brown, Joel. (2016, January 9).

38 Memorable Henry Ford Quotes. Addicted2success.
https://addicted2success.com/quotes/38-memorable-henry-ford-quotes/

41 Edison, Thomas A. brainyquote.com https://www.brainyquote.com/quotes/
thomas_a_edison_149049

42 Tutu, Desmond. Quotable quotes. Goodreads.com
https://www.goodreads.com/
quotes/7424-if-you-are-neutral-in-situations-of-injustice-you-have

43 Morey, Pete. (2019, March 13) 45 Things to know about Marvin Gaye's song,
"What's Going On?"Cbc.ca https://www.cbc.ca/music/read/45-things-you-need-
to-know-about-marvin-gaye-s-what-s-going-on-1.5054267

44 Churchill, Winston. Brainyquote.com https://www.brainyquote.com/quotes/
winston_churchill_156899

45 Editors, History.com. (2020, January 1). The Great Migration.
History.com https://www.history.com/topics/black-history/great-migration

46 Weissert, Will. (2020, August 21). In moving speech, boy says
Biden helped him overcome stutter. Apnews.com https://apnews.
com/30951d24b0dab8b9ced01704d8ee9f2c

47 Keller, Helen. (N.d.). BrainyQuote.com. https://www.brainyquote.com/
citation/quotes/helen_keller_164579

48 Tan, Amy. (N.d.)
Goodreads.com https://www.goodreads.com/
quotes/11530-if-you-can-t-change-your-fate-change-your-attitude

49 Bitchin, Bob. (2017, June 16). The Real Bob Bitchin. Soundingonline.com
https://www.soundingsonline.com/features/the-real-bob-bitchin

50 Churchill, Winston, (2013, March 13). Winston Churchill Quotes. www.
brainyquote.com
https://www.brainyquote.com/quotes/winston_churchill_104164

51 Adler, Alfred. (N.d.) goodreads.com
https://www.goodreads.com/
quotes/776552-seeing-with-the-eyes-of-another-listening-with-the-ears

52 Goleman, Daniel. (N.d.) brainyquote.com https://www.brainyquote.com/quotes/daniel_goleman_585884

53 Polacco, Patricia. (2018, September 11) penquinrandomhouse.com https://www.penguinrandomhouse.com/books/554606/holes-in-the-sky-by-patricia-polacco/

54 Bright Drops. (n.d.) Beautiful Audrey Hepburn Quotes to Fuel Your Soul. Brightdrops.com https://brightdrops.com/audrey-hepburn-quotes

55 McKissack, Patricia C., (2019, January, 8). Penguinrandomhouse.com https://www.penguinrandomhouse.com/books/112100/what-is-given-from-the-heart-by-patricia-c-mckissack-illustrated-by-april-harrison/

56 DeShannaon, Jackie, Myers, Randy and Holiday, Jimmy. (1969) En.winkipedia.org https://en.wikipedia.org/wiki/Put_a_Little_Love_in_Your_Heart

57 Lewis, John (N.D.) Quotable Quotes. Goodreads.com https://www.goodreads.com/quotes/1288239-you-cannot-be-afraid-to-speak-up-and-speak-out

58 Coles, Robert. (2000, January 1). Scholastic Amazon.com https://www.amazon.com/Story-Ruby-Bridges-Robert-Coles/dp/0590439685/ref=asc_df_0590439685/?tag=hyprod-20&linkCode=df0&hva-did=459515588584&hvpos=&hvnetw=g&hvrand=16430593607615023 96&h-vpone=&hvptwo=&hvqmt=&hvdev=c&hvdvcmdl=&hvlocint=&hvloc-phy=9007510&hvtargid=pla-948613825372&psc=1

59 Lawton, Kim. (2004, January 16). John Lewis Extended Interview. Pbs.org https://www.pbs.org/wnet/religionandethics/2004/01/16/january-16-2004-john-lewis-extended-interview/2897/

60 Klein, Christopher. (2020, July 18) How Selma's Bloody Sunday Became a Turning Point in the Civil Rights Movement. History.com https://www.history.com/news/selma-bloody-sunday-attack-civil-rights-movement

61 Lewis, John. (N.D.) azquotes.com https://www.azquotes.com/quote/669894

62 Day, Andrea. (2015) Album: Cheers to the fall en.wikipedia https://en.wikipedia.org/wiki/Andra_Day

63 Hutyra, Hannah. (N.D.). 114 Confucius Quotes That Represent Doctrine Keepinspiringme.com https://www.keepinspiring.me/confucius-quotes/

64 Golenbock, Peter. (1992, August 17) Scholastic.com

https://www.scholastic.com/teachers/books/teammates-by-peter-golenbock/

65 Robinson, Sharon. (2001) Jackie's Nine. Scholastic abebooks.com https://www.abebooks.com/products/isbn/9780439385503?cm_mmc=ggl-_-COM_DSAETAFEED_Trade-_-naa-_-naa&gclid=Cj0KCQjw1qL6BRCm ARIsADV9JtY4TBNzXTrTY1JrsL69KufKYFVsucTqHWw6yacfsimTcGam mnK-nQkaArAzEALw_wcB

66 Robinson, Jackie (n.d.) Quotetab.com
https://www.quotetab.com/quotes/by-jackie-robinson

67 Sasson, Remz. When One Door Closes Another Door Opens. Successconsciousness.com https://www.successconsciousness.com/blog/success/when-one-door-closes-another-door-opens/

68 Brumbeau, Jeff. (2001, March1). Amazon.com
https://www.amazon.com/Quiltmakers-Gift-Jeff-Brumbeau/dp/0439309107

69 Weatherly, Amy Herviewfromhome.com https://herviewfromhome.com/?s=some+people+could+be+given&submit=

70 Hanh, Thich Nhat (n.d.) treasurequotes.com
https://www.treasurequotes.com/quotes/
the-present-moment-is-filled-with-joy-and-happ

71 Williamson, Tina. (2018, June 13). How to Teach Mindfulness To Kids of Any age.
Mindfulmazing.com
https://www.mindfulmazing.com/how-to-teach-mindfulness-to-kids/

72 Berle, Milton. Quotetab.com.
https://www.quotetab.com/quote/by-milton-berle/
laughter-is-the-best-medicine-in-the-world

73 Marvelous, Mrs. Maisel, (2017-present) en.wikipedia.org
https://en.wikipedia.org/wiki/The_Marvelous_Mrs._Maisel

74 M*A*S*H, (1972-1983) CBS
https://en.wikipedia.org/wiki/M*A*S*H_(TV_series)

75 Bowker, Brittany. (2020, July 14). Jimmy Fallon Hosts New York Governor Andrew Cuomo during first show back in studio. Bostonglobe.com
https://www.bostonglobe.com/2020/07/14/nation/jimmy-fallon-welcomes-new-york-governor-andrew-cuomo-during-first-show-back-studio/

76 Li, William MD. (2019)

Drwilliwm.com https://drwilliamli.com/book-li/

77 Multiple Myeloma, Mayo Clinic. Mayoclinic.org.
https://www.mayoclinic.org/diseases-conditions/multiple-myeloma/
symptoms-causes/syc-20353378

78 Learning and the Adolescent Mind. What if all students...?
Learningandtheadolescentmind.com
http://learningandtheadolescentmind.org/home.html

79 Smith, Katie Milway. (2008, February 8). One Hen: How One Small Load
Made a Big Difference. Goodreads.com https://www.goodreads.com/book/
show/2715397-one-hen

80 Onehen.org https://www.onehen.org

81 Choi, Yangsook. (2003, October 14). Dragonfly Books penguinrandomhouse.
com
https://www.penguinrandomhouse.com/books/27340/
the-name-jar-by-yangsook-choi-illustrated-by-the-author/

82 Kids, Lonely Planet. (2015, October 1). Amazon.com
https://www.amazon.com/dp/B016PJQPUI/ref=rdr_kindle_ext_tmb

83 Songland. (2020, April 13). Live Animals, Universal Television
Alternative Studio
Nbc.com https://www.nbc.com/songland

84 Village, The (2019, March 19) nbc.com
https://www.nbc.com/the-village

85 Teachers, Pay Teachers teachesrpayteachers.com
https://www.teacherspayteachers.com/?gclid=Cj0KCQjw-af6BRC5ARIsAAL-
PIlUz9c51iNOt0IFBo9nDCZfe9DsSa79FAWk9Fwu86baM5LIafMqf7AcaAqe-
TEALw_wcB

86 McGill, Bryant H. Brainyquote.com
https://www.brainyquote.com/quotes/bryant_h_mcgill_168276

87 Eger, Edith Dr. (2018). Dreditheger.com https://dreditheger.com/the-choice/

88 Einstein, Albert (2016, May 28). Quoteinvestigator.com
https://quoteinvestigator.com/2016/05/28/not-facts/

89 Emily. (2017, April 10). How to Empower Primary Students Using
Accountable Talk. Educationtothecore.com https://educationtothecore.
com/2017/04/using-accountable-talk/

90 Coelho, Paulo. (2019, October 25) 21 Inspiring Paulo Quotes for Entrepreneurs
Paulcoelho.com https://paulocoelhoblog.
com/2019/10/25/21-inspiring-paulo-coelho-quotes-for-entrepreneurs-2/
91 Dweck, Carol Dr. (2007) Dr. Dweck's research growth mindset changed education forever. Mindsetworks.com
https://www.mindsetworks.com/science/
92 Obama, Barack. (2020, May 16). Obama's High School Virtual Graduation Speech.
Nytimes.com https://www.nytimes.com/2020/05/16/us/obama-graduation-speech-transcript.html
93 Emerson, Ralph Waldo. (n.d.) inspiringquotes.us
https://www.inspiringquotes.us/author/1171-ralph-waldo-emerson
94 Waldorf, Sarah and Stephan, Annelisa. (2020, March 30).
Getty Artworks Recreated with Household Items by Creative Geniuses the World Over. Blogs.getty.eduhttps://blogs.getty.edu/iris/getty-artworks-recreated-with-household-items-by-creative-geniuses-the-world-over/
95 Voyager, Boston. (2018 August 14). Meet Jen Pepper of the Chatty Press in North Shore bostonvoyager.com http://bostonvoyager.com/interview/meet-jen-pepper-chatty-press-north-shore/
96 Pepper, Jen. (2011). The Chatty Press- Custom Design Co.chattypress.com
https://chattypress.com/about-jen/
97 Fair, Molly. (2010) Organizing To End All Forms of Detention, Criminalization, and Surveillance. Communityjusticeexchange.org. https://www.communityjusticeexchange.org
98 Talk Killing of George Floyd. (2020, May 25). En.wikipedia.org
https://en.wikipedia.org/wiki/Killing_of_George_Floyd
99 Parents Scholastic. (2018, November 19) Scholastic Book Fairs Bookfairs.scholastic.com
https://bookfairs.scholastic.com/bookfairs/landing-page.html
100 New York Times Upfront discountmagazines.com https://www.discount-mags.com/magazine/new-york-times-upfront?a=bads&offer=bads&msclkid=d-1b71c2516851da963e0437504501b66&utm_source=bing&utm_medium=cpc&utm_campaign=DiscountMags.com%20Search&utm_term=New%20York%20

Times%20Upfront%20magazine&utm_content=New%20York%20Times%20 Upfront%20Magazine%20Subscription

101 Science in School The European Journal for Science Teachers. Scienceinschool.com https://www.scienceinschool.org

102 Howell, Elizabeth. (2020, February 24). NASA's Real "Hidden Figures". Space.com https://www.scienceinschool.org

103 Scholastic. Scholastic ART. Classroommagazines.scholastic.com https://classroommagazines.scholastic.com/promotion/art.html?psch=CM/ ps/2017/Google/txtl/Art/CM|Brand|Magazines|Exact/scholastic%20 art/61746834929/e/DedicatedHeadline/Scholastic%20Classroom%20 Magazines%20946-276-7123/&k_clickid=_kenshoo_clickid_&promo_ code=3156&gclid=Cj0KCQjw-af6BRC5ARIsAALPIlWovqXOyMg1qu-Ke-0toAwxggz7SbGcuCsm7Fq9eB_j7W2mfuIVUvDIaAvJgEALw_wcB

104 Franklin, Benjamin. Brainyquote.com https://www.brainyquote.com/quotes/ benjamin_franklin_383997

105 Berger, Melvin. (1996, January 1) The Restless Earth: Ranger Rick Science Spectacular amazon.com https://www.amazon.com/ Restless-Earth-Student-Science-Spectacular/dp/1567842372

106 McAnulty, Stacy. Earth: My First 4.54 Billion Years (Part One) Stacymcnaulty.com http://www.stacymcanulty.com/picture-books

107 STEAMS. Steampoweredfamily.com https://www.steampoweredfamily.com/ education/what-is-stem/

108 New York (2020, April 26). 16 -Year old Bronx Student Gains Thousands of Tik Tok Followers Through Tutoring newyork.cbslocal.com https://newyork.cbslocal.com/2020/04/26/tiktok-tutor-alexis-loveras/

109 Tensley, Brandon and Stracqualursi, Veronica. (2020, July 31) Breaking down the significance of John Lewis' funeral service Cnn.com https://www.cnn.com/2020/07/31/politics/john-lewis-atlanta-funeral-service/index.html

110 Dys, Andrew. (2015, June 24). Rock Hill's Elwin Wilson, Georgia congressman John Lewis showed racists can change. Heraldonline.com https://www.heraldonline.com/news/local/news-columns-blogs/andrew-dys/article25437448.html

111 Lewis, John (2017) Across That Bridge A Vision for Change and the Future of America. Barnsandnoble.com https://www.barnesandnoble.com/w/across-that-bridge-john-lewis/1125785623

112 Office of the Governor. (2020, July 28). RI.gov https://www.ri.gov/press/view/38956

113 Operation HOPE operationhope.org https://operationhope.org

114 Markle. We Stand With Others to Condemn Racism, Discrimination and Injustice
Markle.org https://www.markle.org

115 Civilian Conservation Corps (1933-1942) en.wikipedia.org https://en.wikipedia.org/wiki/Civilian_Conservation_Corps

116 Keller, Helen brainyquote .com https://www.brainyquote.com/quotes/helen_keller_101340

117 Lehrman, Lewis E. (2017, February 9). "Stand Firm": Lincoln's Advice to a Nurse, the Union and Himself wjs.com https://www.wsj.com/articles/stand-firm-lincolns-advice-to-a-nurse-the-union-and-himself-1486686456

118 Obama, Barack. (2020, August 20). Transcript: Barack Obama's DNC Speech Cnn.com https://www.cnn.com/2020/08/19/politics/barack-obama-speech-transcript/index.html

119 Hastie, William. What is Democracy? Facinghistory.org https://www.facing-history.org/resource-library/what-democracy

120 Wilkie, Christina. (2020, August 17) Michelle Obama tells "the cold hard truth" in a searing DNC keynote speech. Cnbc.com https://www.cnbc.com/2020/08/17/michelle-obama-tells-cold-hard-truth-in-a-searing-dnc-keynote-speech.html

121 Watch Market (2020, August, 20). Joe Biden's speech to the Democratic convention full text. Marketwatch.com https://www.marketwatch.com/story/joe-bidens-speech-to-the-democratic-convention-full-text-2020-08-20

122 Woodson, Jacqueline. (2012) Each Kindness barnsandnoble.com https://www.barnesandnoble.com/w/each-kindness-jacqueline-woodson/1109324628

123 Lewis, John, (2020, July 30) John Lewis column: Together, you can redeem the soul of our nation Orlandosentinel.com https://www.orlandosentinel.com/featured/

sns-nyt-op-john-lewis-posthumous-column-20200730-biulev7tt5cavhz2w6d-cpood24-story.html

124 Williamson, Jean (2020, August 25).

Insider.com.

https://www.insider.com/
jacob-blakes-mother-we-need-healing-powerful-speech-about-son-2020-8-25

125 India.com staff (2020, July 16) International Nelson Mandela Day 2020: His History and Significance Day india.com

https://www.india.com/festivals-events/international-nelson-mande-la-day-2020-history-and-significance-of-the-day-4086301/